Christopher Ness, Titus Oates

The Devils Patriarck

A full and impartial account of the notorious life of this present Pope of Rome,

Innocent the 11th

Christopher Ness, Titus Oates

The Devils Patriarck
*A full and impartial account of the notorious life of this present Pope of Rome, Innocent the
11th*

ISBN/EAN: 9783337100797

Printed in Europe, USA, Canada, Australia, Japan

Cover: Foto ©Lupo / pixelio.de

More available books at **www.hansebooks.com**

Innocut the 11 Pope of Rome

London Printed for J. Dunton at y.ᶜ black Raven in y.ᵉ
Poultrey.

THE
DEVILS PATRIARCK,
OR
A Full and Impartial Account
Of the
NOTORIOUS LIFE
Of this Prefent
𝕻𝖔𝖕𝖊 𝖔𝖋 𝕽𝖔𝖒𝖊
INNOCENT the 11th.

Wherein is *newly* Difcovered his *Rife and Reign* ; The *Time and Manner* of Ĥis being chofen Pope ; His Prime Procetfion , Confecration and Coronation ; The *Splendour* and *Grandeur* of his Court ; His molt *Eminent* and *Gainful* Cheats, by which he Gulls the *filly* People ; His *Secret* and *Open* Tranfactions with the Papifts in *England,Scotland, France* and *Ireland*, and other Protefant Countreys to this *very* day ; Together with the *Reft* of the Hellifh Policies and Infamous Actions of his wicked Life.

Written by an *Eminent Pen* to Revive the Remembrance of the *almoft* forgotten Plot againft the Life of his Sacred Majefty and the Protetant Religion.

𝕰𝖓𝖙𝖊𝖗𝖊𝖉 𝖆𝖈𝖈𝖔𝖟𝖉𝖎𝖓𝖌 𝖙𝖔 𝕺𝖟𝖉𝖊𝖗. ·

LONDON, Printed for *John Dunton* at the Black-*Raven* in the *Poultrey.* 1683.

THE
PREFACE
TO THE
READER.

Candid and Curteous Reader,

Hen a *suddain and surprizing* In-
vasion *is made upon us by a*
Foreign Power, *every Right-
thinking Mind cannot but Judg*
it *high time to* Fire our Beacons. Æsops
Witty Wisdom, (*in his* Fable of the Shepherd-Boy, *that cry'd out falsly, as well as
frequently*, [The Wolf comes, the Wolf
comes, Help, Help.] *to the People*,) *hath
in the* Apologues Moral *a very shrewd* Congruity, *with our present Case, though there
wants not also some* Disparity.

(1.) *The* Congruity *consists in these parti-
culars*,

First, *Every Shepherd should be careful to
preserve the Flock committed to his Charge ;
so ought every* Mystical, *as well as the* Literal Shepherd, (*whether* τεόϕυλος aut Emixis
π⑨, Young *or* Old,) *to be*.

B   Secondly,

Secondly, *Both ought to cry out of* Probable *and* Approaching Dangers. *It was not at all Improbable, that the Wolf was a coming, becauſe he us'd frequently to do ſo.* •

Thirdly, *When* Dangers *are both* Probable *and* Approaching, (*for 'tis the Nature of the* Beaſt *to* worry the Sheep,) *then 'tis the Du-y of* Both, *not only to* Cry out, *but to* Crave Help *from the* Peoples *Hands, yea to quicken up* their *Aſſiſtance with ſtrong and Reiterated Outcrys, That the* Abaddon, (*a bad one indeed,*) *the* Apollyon, *or Devouring Beaſt, is juſt a coming.*

- Fourthly, *All Hands are few enough to* Help the Lord *againſt this* Mighty, (*yea in the* Romiſh *phraſe,* Almighty,) Beaſt.

Fifthly, *All private Works muſt be left, (* both *in* City *and* Countrey,) *for ſtopping the ſtrong* Current *of a* Publick *and* Common Calamity.

·· Sixthly, *As the* Sheep *of* Æſops Shepherd *were* Grazing, [in eminentiori Loco,] *upon* Lofty Mountains , *yet not* Inacceſſible *to the* Wolf : *So the* Sheep, *which* Goſpel-Shepherds *are feeding , and which the* Romiſh Wolf *would Worry, are likewiſe* Grazing *upon the* Holy-Hill *of* Zion, *the* higheſt of all Hills , *yet not ſo high , but , when the Sins of the Sheep do open a paſſage, becomes* Acceſſible *to the* Wolf *alſo. Where the Beaſt hath*

been

been before, Treading down the Green Pa-
ftures, and fouling the Refidue with his
foul Feet, *he hath fome hope for returning thither again, efpecially, feeing the* Neft-Egg *of*
Romifh *Reliques is ftill-left behind to encou-
rage his Return :* Bloody Bifhop Bonner *could*
once Briskly *Brag,* Such as like to Sup our
Broth, we will make them love to Eat our
Beef too : *God grant us a good Deliverance
from fuch Barbarous Butchers , and Beaftly
Butcheries, from that* Brutifh People, Skilful
to Deftroy.

(2.) *As to the* Difparity,

Firft, *The Outcry of* Æfops *Shepherd-Boy
was only,* [Joci gratià,] *a falfe* Holloe *for
Sport-fake, a Boyifh-Trick, playing the Wag
with the Mafters of the Sheep, to whom he
was but an Hireling-Servant : But the Outcry
of our Shepherds have been ever more* Real
and Serious, *from the many Effays and Attempts, which* Rome *has really made to Reduce (as* Colemans *Phrafe is,)* this Northern Herefie *to her Obedience :* She *hath all
along, ever fince the* Reformation of Religion *here, with all her* Fraud *and* Force, *with
all* Her Craft *and* Cruelty *endeavoured to re-
enter with her* Deformation *of it, and to Re-
cover both her* Neft, *and her* Neft-Egg, *from
which fhe was forced.*

The Preface

Secondly, *Our Outcry hath not been made by some one* Novice, *or of many* Novices *only, but also of the most Grave, most Judicious, and most Thinking Discerning* Fathers *of the Sheepfold, who, with* Moses, *could espye the very first Outgoings of Wrath, and, with* Elijah *could Observe a Black Cloud, though no bigger than a Mans Hand :   All these at Sundry Times , and in Divers Manners, have* όμοθυμαδὸν, *as with one Mouth Sounded Loud Alarms.*

Thirdly, *Though those call'd in to be Assistants against the Wolf, in the* Fable, [nihil esse comperiebant,] *found nothing of real Danger. Yet those call'd together to Assist against* the Wolf *of* Romes *Incursions, have upon undenyable grounds found out a Real Danger, Witness* His Majesty *and* Privy-Councils Reiterated Proclamations , *the* Unanimous Votes of Four Successive Parliaments, *(all call'd upon for their Assistants, &c.) The* Forms of Prayer, Composed *and* Imposed *by the* Bishops, *for the Fast appointed by Authority, upon the Account of the* Popish Plot, *as also the Murder of* Justice Godfrey, *and the Just Execution of some Grand Conspirators.*

Fourthly, *The Sheep-worrying Beast in the Fable, is expresly call'd a* Wolf *only , though there be other Beasts as obnoxious to* Sheep. **But**

But this Molock *of* Rome *is such a Bloudy Beast, as no Name could sufficiently express his Bloud-Thirstiness.* Hereupon (1.) Daniel *calls the* First Beast, (*or* Assyrian Empire,) *a* Lyon. *The* Second, (*the* Medo-Persian,) *a* Bear. *The* Third, (*the* Grecian,) *a* Leopard. *But the* Fourth, *to wit*, (*the* Roman Empire,) *he calls a* Beast *in general,* (*without any name,*) *as if* Exceeding, (*as well as* Including,) *the Savage Nature of all the Three former,* Dan. 7. 4, 5, 6, 7, 23. (2.) John *also*, (*as well as* Daniel,) *calls him a* Beast *in the general,* (without, *because above any Name,*) *yet makes he him a Monstrous Beast , Compounded of all the Three Beasts aforesaid , as having the* Feet of a Bear, *the* Mouth of a Lyon, Himself like a Leopard, *and* the Dragon giving him Power, Revel. 13. 2. *And though* Rome Heathen *hath done much against* Chrifts Sheep, Slaying its Thousands, *yet* Rome Anti-Chriftian *hath done more, and far outdone it in* Slaying its Ten Thousands : *So that this* Beaft, (*above all Names*,) *is a* Beaft *with a Witness, an Hyperbolical* Behemoth, *as if many Beasts made up One*, (*so the* Hebrew Plural Feminine *signifies,*) *far beyond the moft Bloud-Thirfty* Wolf, *yea the moft Savage* Cannibal, *for Eating the Flesh and Drinking the Bloud of* Poor Proteftants,

The Preface

even to an high Inebriation, as the Sequel will more fully Demonstrate: *Take but this Taft here*, *'Tis credibly Related, That in the fpace of Eight Hundred Years*, *this* Monftrous Beaft, *(who hath all Cruelties Concentred in him,) hath been the Death of Twelve Millions of Chriftians.* Idæa Reform. Antichr. Tom. 1. Part 2. Sect. 2. Cap. 6. *To Inftance only one Specimen of this* Pourtray'd Beaft *in this place, to wit,* Pope Julius the Second, *(who was turn'd up Trump, and Triumph'd in the Chair of Peftilence, in the Fifteenth Century) that made a fhift to Worry (in Seven Years fpace of his Papacy) no fewer than Seven Hundred Thoufand* Sheep. See Baleus de Actis Rom. pontif. lib. 7. *'Tis one of* Luthers *Divine Raptures, that* Cain *(the Firft-Born of the Devils Patriarks) fhall be Murdering his Brother* Abel *to the end of the World : and the Older he groweth, the more Blood-Thirfty he becometh* : *This* Romifh Runnet *(as is commonly faid of the* Common *in Dairy Houfes) the Older it is, it grows fo much the* Stronger. *If the* Beaft *were fo Bloudy in that Century aforementioned, how much more may he be expected in* this prefent Pope. *Seeing* [Morfus moribundæ Beftiæ funt maximè mortiferi,] *The laft Bitings of a Dying Beaft are moftly moft Deadly : and whether this be yet paft,* Sub Judice

lis

lis eft, 'tis *a matter of Controverfie, and if not , I would ask my* Countrymen Prote-ftants, *Is this a Beaft fit to be* Courted into England? *which is indeed the Bloudy* Scar-let-Colour'd Whore, *that better deferveth to* be Carted out of it, *and out of the World alfo.*

Fifthly, *It doth not appear, that the* Wolf *in the* Fable *was ever reftrained from any Attempts by thofe frequent outcries for Affiftance, feeing the Report of his approaching was falfe until the laft.* But this Beaft of Rome *hath had many fignal and fingular reftraints by* King *and* Parliament, &c. *But above all, by an Invifible and an Over-ruling Hand; fo that fhe hath been conftrained to alter her Methods, and to take new Meafures, Foifting her dead Brats into the* Bofom of Innocent Proteftants, *which though it need not the Wifdom of a* Solomon *to Difcover, yet requireth it the Power of a* Parliament *more fully to Determine, in a way of Vindicative Juftice.*

Sixtly *and* Laftly, *I wifh with all my Soul, that there may be found more* Difparity *than* Congruity *in the* Cataftrophe *and Clofure of the* Fable, *as Relating to our prefent* Cafe. *The* Apologue *indeed concludeth thus; that whereas the* Husbandmen *had been oft abufed by the falfe Alarms of the* Boy, *leaving their Ploughs ftanding Idle in the Field, to deliver the Sheep*

whe

The Preface

when there was no Danger, then the Wolf coming in good earneſt, the Boy cries out, but
was not believed by them, whom he had ſo oft
deceived, hereupon the Wolf prevails againſt
the Boy, Worries the Sheep without reſiſtance,
Gluts himſelf with their Fleſh and Bloud, and
eſcapes away ſcotfree, without ſo much as a
blow for that unparallel'd miſcheif: The
Moral of this laſt part is, as Solomon, with
his wonderful Wiſdom, helps us to Interpret it,
ſaying, Woe be to that Land, that hath
[ὁμοίᾳ Ἀζῶν, ovium Paſtorem]no wiſer than
a Child, Eccl. 10.16. Alas, He is not able, (though
never ſo willing)to Deliver his Flock, &c. Solomon ſaith alſo, But in multitude of Councellors there is ſafety, Prov. 11.14. This Shepherds Boy had ſo much Wit in him, as to call
in more helping Hands to his own, though he did
oft cry ſo Childiſhly, and at laſt (through his
own fooliſh fraud) fruitleſly without ſucceſs.
We have had many loud Alarms Trumpeted
out, crying, [The Romiſh Wolf is coming,
Help, Help,] and though none of the many
have been falſe outcries, as before, yet would to
God the Helping Husbandmen may not
(through ſo many Diſappointments) grow weary of Appearing, ſo let the Devouring Beaſt
have his Blond-Thirſty Luſt ſatiated upon the
Proteſtant-Sheep, and all this without any
reſiſtance and oppoſition. But though this
                                        Apologue

to the Reader.

Apologue *of* Æfops *be thus fignificantly fuitable in its* Moral, *yet have we a* Divine Parable *(to Wit, that of* Jothams, *Judg.* 9.) *that infinitely Tranfcends it in its fignal and fingular Signature as to our prefent Calamitous Condition. Bloudy* Abimeleck (*a bafe* Baftard) *Ufurps the Kingdom, which by fubtle practifing upon his* Kinsfolk *and the* Men of Shechem *he* craftily compaffed, *and (by the help of his vile Vagrants and Villanous Followers, Hired with the Treafure of* Baal-Berith *) as* cruelly conftituted *the Foundation of it, in Murdering (like a bloudy Tyrant*) *Seventy Innocent, and all Legitimate Competitors to make his way to the Throne,* Good Jotham *onely efcaping,* He *takes the boldnefs (notwithftanding his Perfonal Danger) to make* his mind (*yea and* Gods *too)* known *to the* Men of Shechem *from the* top of Mount Gerizim (*that* Bleffing, *not* Mount Ebal *that* Curfing Mountain) *Before he took to his Heels, and fled from the Tyrant. As this Sacred* Apologue of Jotham's, (*who, though but a young Man, was* vir bonus, di-. cendi peritus, *a good Man, and a* good Orator, *one that* could declare his Mind fitly, *and* durft do it Freely, *being* [θεόπνευστος] *Infpired of Gods Spirit) doth therefore far (I fay) Tranfcend the aforefaid Fable of* Æfop, *fo it* more highly *merits a larger Defcant upon it, were I not bound up to the* Narrow
Limits

The Preface

Limits of a Short and yet Succinct Preface. *Hereupon, all that I am Allowed to Add, is, to let the Ingenious Reader know, that the He-brew Doctors do Understand by the Fig-Tree in the Parable, Renowned* Deborah *their* Delive-reſs, *as by the* Olive-tree Othniel, *or* Ehud, *and by the* Fruitful Vine, Gideon *with his Numerous Off-ſpring ; what is meant by the* Bramble *needs not much Explication, it being not a* Tree, *but a* Shrub *(the Product of* Gods Curſe upon the Earth, *Gen.* 3. 17, 18. *)* Prickly, Barren, Baſe, Abject, *good for no-thing, but to* Stop Gaps, *or* Kindle a Fire : Abimeleck *was a* Right Bramble *indeed, who grew in the baſe* Hedg-Row *of a Contemptible* Concubine *, who horribly ſcratch'd and drew Bloud to purpoſe, when once he had (by the help of* Baal-Beriths *Treaſure) ſcrambl'd up to a Dominion over* Iſrael, *whereunto he was* Handed *by his* hired *Beggerly* Raſcals, *and* Debauched Deſperado's : *The* ἐπιμύϑιον *or* Moral *Hereof (as to us) is obvious to every common Underſtanding, and neither the* Ex-plication, *nor the* Application *is any matter of Difficulty: I ſhall therefore conclude my Præ-liminary part with this pathetical* Epiphone-ma, *as a* Golden Key *to open the* Myſtery *of* Iniquity : *Oh* England, England, *Thou haſt had thy Delivering* Deborah (Queen Elizabeth) *who ſaved thee in Gods Hand from*

the

the Cúrſed Canaanites, *that delt cruelly with thee in the* Marian Days, *Thou haſt alſo had thy* Othniels, Ehuds *who did ſtab the* **Red** Letter Cauſe *with their very* Pens (*as* King James) *excellently and unanſwerably Accom-pliſhed, though* he *was but* left handed *for the Sword, having for his* Motto [Rex pacifi-cus] *which one wittely Engliſhed* [put up thy Dagger Jamy] *And ſome Abuſive wits limn'd his Picture with a* Padlock *upon his Sword, yet his* Learned Writing *did ſo effec-tually vindicate his undoubted Right againſt* Pope Paul the Fifth, *that there was no need of* Martial Warring (Cedant Arma Togæ, *&c.) There was no cccaſion for* Mars, *where* Minerva *was his* Bellona, *which made his* Un-Holineſs *Decline the Encounter :* Thou *haſt likewiſe had thy* Gideon *with a fruitful Ofspring, ſtout Aſſertors of the Reformed Re-ligion, ſhouldſt thou? now forſake the* Fitneſs, *the* Fatneſs, *and the* Fruitfulneſs *of thy Truly Noble* Figtree, Olive *and* Vine (*which indeed hath* cheered God and Man) *and at laſt em-brace a* Baſe Bramble, *that* exotick, dry, empty, Saples Kex *and* Weed *of a* Forraign Power, *to wit, that of the* Man of Sin, *the* Son of Perdition *and the* wicked one, *which is the threefold* Black-Brand, *wherewith* An-tichriſt *is Stigmatized by the* Holy Ghoſt. *How far this threefold Character agreeth with*

the

the Pope ; See *the* Man of Sin, *lib.* 1, *chap.* 4. Foulis Hiftory *of* Romifh Treafons *and* U-furpations *per totum*, *and* Nefles Difco-very *of* Antichrift, *pag.* 55. *to* 63. &c. *what their own Authours Report of* them *may be beft believed :* That this Babylonifh Brat *is a* Baftard *like the* Bramble Abimeleck, *and and not* Legitimate, *or Heaven-born, their own very Creatures are conftrained to Confefs.*

As Firft, Platina, *who was the* Pope's *own Secretary, and Keeper of the* Vatican- Library , *yea a Writer by Commiffion from* Pope Sixtus *the* Fourth.

Secondly , Benno Ufpergenfis , *one of* Romes *own Cardinals.*

Thirdly, *And* Math. Parifienfis *a* Bene-dictin Monk *of the Monaftary of St.* Albans *here in* England, *All thefe three (none of them writing out of Prejudice, fo they would have bewray'd their own Neft, but Imparti-ally and in Truth) doe Unanimoufly Defcribe the* Popes *to be Limbs of the Devil ; the laft of which Relates, How* [Diabolus, & Infe-rorum Contubernium, *&c.] that the* De-vil *and All his Hellifh* Crew *Wrote Gratulato-ry Letters to the* Pope *and his* Clergy, for fending more Souls to Hell, than ever went before, *Math. Paris Hift. Angl. Guil. Conqueft. Anno.* 1072. *pag.* 10. *Yea none of them can deny, but that fome of the* Popes *fold themfelves*

to

to the Deuil *for their obtaining of the Popedom by his Craft.* Therefore the Men of Shechem or England *need no* Jotham *to Proclaim to them,* (*seeing the very* Romanists *themselves say enough*) *that if* in Truth ye Anoint this Pope to have Dominion over you, *and Return again to* put your Trust in his Shadow, *ye will be not cnely Notoriously disapointed in your* Shelter *under such a* Shadow (*for the* Bramble-Bush *cannot yeild any good Shade ; the silly Sheep flying to it for shelter, are sure to lose part of their* Fleece, *if not of their Flesh too*) But *also a* Fire *will flow fiercely forth from this* Base Bramble *to Devour you, and your tallest Cedars : This one* Terræ-filius *or* Bastard *will destroy all your true-born Sons : He that hath but half an eye, may* both see *and* foresee *the Matchless mischeifs that must be its Consequences, which they that are so Hot for a* Popish Succeſſour (*while they yet profeſs themselves to be good* Proteſtants) *dce not Duly and Truly Conſider. But I must not detain you too loug in the* Porch, *for fear of your catching cold. Having Diſpatched the* Prologue, *conſiſting of a Double* Apologue, (*which may be further Illuſtrated and Applyed in the* Epilogue) *Let me now hand you to the Houſe it ſelf, wherein you may take a plain Proſpeƈt of this* preſent Pope *limn'd to the life in his Right Red Vermilion Colours.*

T. O.

The Notorious

LIFE

Of this prefent

POPE of *ROME,*

[*INNOCENT*, XI.]

THis prefent *Pope* of *Rome* was *Cardinal Odefchalchi* of *Come* in the *Dutchy* of *Millaine*, when called to the *Roman-Chair*, whether we wrong him in reckoning him among the Bafe Brambles of the Curfed Earth, is the [το ζητηθμον] *Poftulatum*, or *Grand Enquiry*. In the General let *Dr. Prideaux* give the Anfwer for me, who Writes a *Compendious Hiftory* of the Lives of all the *Popes*, and after he hath paft the *Patriarchs*, (and the tollerable Popes) *He* begins at *Anno Dom:* 606. with U*furping Nimrods*, (a worfe Name than *Brambles*) and Reckons *Thirty Eighth Popes* (*Cruel Hunters all,*) from that Year, to 847.

The

The *First* of which Black Bed-Roll, was *Boniface* the *Third*, and *Leo* the *Fourth* was the Last.

His next Rank were (as he Stiles them) *Rank Luxurious Sodomites*, whereof *He* Reckons *Forty*, from the Year 855. to 996. the *First* of them was *Pope John* the *Eighth* (in plain *English*, *Pope Joan*, the *Rank Whore*, which God would have, to Declare to all the World, That the Church of *Rome* is the *Apocalyptick* Whore,) and the Last of that Number was *Gregory* the *Fifth*.

His *Third* fort of *Popes*, from the Year 999. to 1240. that He prefents to our View, are another Bundle of *Forty Popes* again, whom He Dignifies with that Honourable Title of *Ægyptian Magicians*; the First of this Black Regiment was *Sylvester* the *Second*, and the Last was *Cælestine* the *Fourth*.

His *Fourth Prospect* of Popes *He* giveth, is another lovely Clufter of Sower Grapes, confifting of *Eight* and *Thirty Popes*, from the Year 1243. to 1503. The Captain whereof is *Innocent* the *Fourth*, and the Lieutenant (that brings up the Rear) is *Pius* the *Third*, All which he Brandeth for a Company of *Devouring Abaddons*, All *Bad-ones* beyond Bounds.

Yet ſtill there be *worſe* behind, [*Occupat extremum Scabies*,] which as ſome do *Engliſh*, not only the *Scab*, but the *Devil* cometh hindermoſt. 'Tis the Divine Doom inflicted upon the *Church of Rome*, as an Apoſtate, to be *waxing worſe* and *worſe*, therefore it may the leſs be wondred at, that the *laſt Claſſis of Popes*, (which are the very *Dregs* of Time,) muſt be the worſt, and thereupon are worthily Stigmatiz'd with the worſt Appellation. The Words of the Reverend Author aforeſaid, Run thus, [after the *Devouring Abaddons*,] To fill up the *Myſtery* and *Meaſure* of *Iniquity*, the *Incurable Babylonians* do next ſtep upon the Stage, [*Curavimus Babylona*, *& non eſt Sanata*, Jerem. 51. 6.] *We would have Cured* Babylon, *but ſhe could not be Cured;* for the reſt of the Men that were not Killed by thoſe Plagues, Repented not of their (1.) *Murthers*; (2.) *Sorceries*, (3.) *Fornications*, (4.) *Thefts*, Revel. 9. 20, 21. This *laſt* and *worſt* Rank reaches from the Year 1503. to this preſent 1683. betwixt which Two Periods the Number of Popes are *Twenty-Five*, (the *feweſt Number* of all the Five Claſſes, yet have the *Fouleſt*, both *Name* and *Nature*) whereof *Julius* the Second leads the Van, and this preſent *Pope*, (the ſubject of our Diſcourſe,) brings up the Rear. C I

I would have given· fome fhort Remarks upon thefe feveral Claffes, (thus dignified and diftinguifhed with thofe Five aforefaid Honourable Titles,) and upon the feveral Popes, as they ftand in Rank and File, under their feveral Banners in every Claffis, had it not been befide my prefent purpofe, and would it not have fwoln this Difcourfe too mnch.   I fhall therefore fatisfie my felf, and the Reader with Two Remarks only.

The *Firft Remark* is, That the Leader of the Van in the Second Rank, is a *Virago* rather than a *Virgo*, a Pope of the *Fæminine Gender*, that Taught Gramarians to Decline *Papa* with *Hæc* not *Hic* : The name of this *Female Pope*, (*John* or *Joan*) both in a Literal and Myftical Senfe, fheweth that *Rome* may well be called the *Whore of Babylon*, *Romifh* Chronologers have not Inferted her Name in the Catalogue of Popes, which *Marianus Scotus* Renders this Reafon· for, [*Propter Turpituidinem Rei*, *& Sexum Muliebrem*,] becaufe the wrong *Gender* would be a Reproach to them.   Wherefore to avoid the like Difgrace, the *Porphiry Chair*, (or Groping-ftool·) was Ordained, *Ubi ab Ultimo Diaccno* , &c.   Where the loweft Deacon muft make the Experiment, &c.   Hence it is, That thefe Popes who

have

have called themfelves [*Johns*] are fo ill
ordered in their common Catalogues, fome
making that *John* which Succeeded [*Adrian*
the Second] in the Year 872. to be *John*
the *Eighth,* and others *John* the *Ninth* : Ingenious *Platina* forequoted, doth only (of
all the *Romanifts*) Recken *Pope Joan* as the
Eighth of the *Johns,* and fo farward : And
'tis proboble enough (faith Dr. *Heylin,* a
Man Fair and Favourable enough) that
God fuffer'd that Proud See of *Rome* to fall
into fuch a profound Reproach, the more
to cut the Coxcombs of the Succeeding
Popes in their Higheft Ruff and Riotings,
and the better to beat down their Eig Brags
of a continued Succeffion, whereof they
are frequently Boafting. As [*Remember*
Lots *Wife*] is a due Caution to us, fo I fee
not why [*Remember Pope* Joan] fhould
not be likewife a true Check to them : The
Truth of this Story, as to matter of Fact,
Mr. *Alexander Cook* (my quondam Prede-
:effour) in his Book of *Pope Joan* hath proved it by Irrefragable Arguments, and hath
moft Induftruoufly batter'd down all the
Objections which the moft Mercurial Wits
of *Rome* could raife againft it. See his Book,
and Dr. *Heylins Cofmography* in Folio the laft
Edition, pag. 107. *&c.* The *Baftard Abime-*
ech aforementioned did Defperately grudg,

that it fhould be faid [*a Woman had Braind
him*] Judg. 9. 54. Sure I am, *this bafe born
Brat of* Rome (the *Head* of the Church)hath
Received (were *He* fenfible) a *Deadly
Wound* by the hands of a Woman likewife,
with this difference only, the *former* was
Active, and Defigning, the *latter* was *Paf-
five*, and never purpofed the Wounding :
'Tis fuch a Reproach to the *Roman* Chair as
will never be wiped off ; this is the *Semira-
mis*, the *Amazoman Queen*, the *She-Captain*,
that ftands in the Front of the *Second* Rank,
to wit, of the *Luxurious Sodomits*.

The *Second Remark* is, concerning *Julio*
the *Second*, who ftands as a *ftout Generaliffi-
mo* of the laft Rank, to wit, of *Incurable
Babylonians*, and *He* is moft fitly placed in
that Station, as having far more of the
Souldier, than of the *Prelate* in Him, keeping *Italy*, all his Popedom, in continual
Wars, and for a pregnant proof, that this
Romifh God, was a *Man of Mettal*, This is
the *Pope*, who paffing over *Tyber-Bridg*,
firft Brandifh'd his Sword, and then threw
his Keys into the River, faying, If *Peters
Keys* would not ferve his Turn, then *Pauls*
Sword fhould do it Home.

Such a Thrafonick Bravado would bet-
ter become *Julius Cæfar* the *Emperour* of
Rome, than *Julius Secundus* the *Bifhop* of
R. me.

Rome. But I have been thinking, that 'tis a
Thoufand pities, Famous *Pope Joan* had
not her Lot in this Laft Rank too, yea, and
(were it not to Dethrone and Difpoffes
this *Heroick Hector*) *She* might have ftood
in the Captains place there, as *She* doth in
the Second Rank, [*Detur digniori*] is the
Rule, She beft deferving it : for where could
that *Whore* of *Babylon* (as above) be better placed ? than among the *Incurable Babylonians,* and where could that *Incurable*
Whore have been better order'd? than in
the Front of that *File* of *Defiled* and *Defile-
ing Beafts.*

However, this *prefent Pope,* Cardinal O-
defchalcho, (who hath chang'd his Name
into *Innocent* the *Eleventh,*) is Reprefented
to our View as ftanding upon the Tail and
Fag-end of thofe *Incurable Babylonians* : We
ufe to fay, Such a perfon as Labors under
a Mortal Incurable Difeafe, hath a [*Mife-
rere Mei Deus,*] writ upon his Door : who
it is, that Writes the *Continuation of* Dr. *Prideaux's Introduction,* I know not, yet he
Writes an *Epitome* of this our Cardinal *Odefchalcho's* publick *Actions* and *Tranfactions,*
fince his coming to be Groped in the *Por-
phyry Chair* : and we are much obliged to
that *Author* (who ever he is) for fixing
this *prefent Pope* under the Head of *Incurable*

Babylonians, but I know not (in all the World) how to Reconcile the *White Chara-cter* that *Author* giveth *him*, and the *Black Title* he fetteth *over him*. The Defcription of his Life there, feems to carry no Congruity with an *Incurable Babylonian*. 'Tis great pi-ty, that any miftaking Candour fhould make fuch a Difparity : but to let that pafs, come we now to give a more full and Impartial Account of his *Rife* and *Begining*, &c. So far as Hiftorians lends any light *hereunto*.

I find that *this Perfon* (fo foon as any Fame found *him*) had his firft noticed Ca-pacity at *Come*, a place of note in the *Dukedom of Millain* in *Italy*, a *Town*, made the more Famous by being the Birth-place of the two *Famous Plinys*, and fituated on the *South*-fide of the *Lacus Larius*, which from this *Town* hath now the name of *Lago di Como*, through this Lake the Ri-ver *Addua* runs; yet (as *Geographers* fay) their two Waters do not mingle : Which two Remarks hath occafion'd in Me *two Wifhes* in this *mans* behalf. The firft is, that as *Pliny* became the more Famous for ftop-ping *Trajan* the Emperour from perfecuting the poor Chriftians in the Empire, by wri-ting elegantly to Him, that He found no greater fault laid to the charge of the per-
                                                          fecuted,

fecuted, fave this, that they did *(Cantus Ante-lucanos canere) fing Pfalms before day*; upon which Letter the perfecution ceafed: So would to God this *prefent' Pope* might write fuch an effectual Letter to the *French King* in the behalf of the poor perfecuted Proteftants in *France,* (fure I am, he can find no worfe faults in them*)* fo ftop the perfecution there, this would make him more *Famous*, than ever the Recovery of his *Regalitys* (he hath been fo long contending for*)* can Render Him : whereas, to be outvy'd by a blind Heathen (fuch was *Pliny)* in fuch a good Work of *Piety* and *Charity* (which are Works highly cryed up at *Rome*) may Render Him for ever *Infa-mous.* Efpecially if *He* be found to pufh it on and promote it, inftead of putting a ftop to it. The *fecond Wifh* is, Oh that this pretended Vicar of Chrift may learn fome Divine Leffon, even from the very *Nature* of his own Country-River, which will not *mingle* its *pure Streams* with the puddle wa-ter of a *corrupted ftanding Lake* : not to play the Huxter in Sophifticating, and Adulterating the truth of the Gofpel, by mingling it with corrupt Traditions. There is certainly moft *Evangelical Doctrine* in that Levitical Law, *thou fhalt not let thy Cattle Gender with a diverfe Kind, thou fhalt not Sow thy*

Field

Field with a mingled Seed, neither shall a Garment mingled of Linnen and Wollen come upon thee] Levit. 19. 19. to shew, that *Miscelanees* in Religious Worship are both *hateful* to *God*, and *hurtful* to *Men* : and not onely the nature of *His River*, but also naturalists do teach Him not to mingle the *Inventions of Men*, with the *Institutions of God*, for they say, that though *Gold* be so · Ductile, as to be willing to mix and incorporate it self with *other Mettals*, save onely with *Latten*, notwithstanding, as to its outward Luftre, it be so like it self : so the true Church (which is call'd a *golden Candlestick*) will not mix or embody her self with the false (commonly called the *Latin*) Church, which stagnateth like a stinking Lake, though she resembleth the *Spouse*, and *sits in the Temple of God*, 2 Thes. 2. 4. but indeed is the *Apocalyptick Whore*, and the most Capital Enemy to the Flock of Christ, in all the laft Ages : This *present Pope*, while he was in his *publick Capacity* (omitting his *private*, as not worth Recording) at this Town of *Come*, went under the name of *Benedict Odefchalci*, of the Title of *Saint Onuphrius* and was created a *Cardinal* under *Pope Innocent* the 10th. *March* the 6th. in the year 1645. Upon which take these *Remarks*.

First,

First, 'Tis not eafie to Affign the Reafon why his proper *prænomen* (that of *Benedict*) fhould become fo difguftful to *Him* as to change it into *Innocent* (the Name of his Predeceflours in the Chair) feeing it was (as it fignifies) a *bleffed* Name, and alfo the Name of fome *Popes* before him, but more of that change of Names afterwards, when we come to his *Popedom*.

Secondly, There may a more probable conjecture be·given for the change of his *Sir-Name*, to wit, *Odefchalcho*, more efpecially when it is Allowable to give an *Italick* Name an *Attick Etymology*, and fo [*nomen quafi notamen*] that *Name* hath an evil found, fent, and fenfe, fignifying (not a *Golden*) but a *Brazen Song*. That which fents and favours of *Brafs* (we ufually fay) is unpleafant to the Palate, and 'tis the more likely this Name might be difguftful to his Palate, feeing his Predeceflour *Sergius the Second*, even quarelled with his own Name, which (before he was *Pope*) was [*Bocca di Porco*] fignifying *Swine-Mouth*, or *Hog-Face*, and thinking that ill-founding Name not fuitable to his Dignity, he therefore changed it. And upon fuch an Honourable Prefident, if *Hog-Face* was fo odious a Name to the former, why might not alfo *Brafs-Face* or *Brazen-Face* (as a *Face of Brafs* is an appro-

approbrious Phrafe amongft us) be odious
to this latter.

Thirdly, As to the Title of Saint *Onuphrius* he was dignified with at *Come*, I fhall
onely fay at this time (though much more
might be added) what Tradition tells us of
this *Onuphrius*, that he was a monkifh Man,
who lived a folitary Life for fixty years, in
which fpace he faw no Man : had our *Odef.*
chalcho Imitated this monkifh *Patroon* , and
trode in this *Pattern's* Steps, he had never become a *Cardinal*, much lefs a *Pope*, unto
which *converfing* with Men, and *conveying*
Kindnefles to them (to oblige their Votes
at Election) are neceffary Ingredients, and,
which he to the utmoft improved.

Fourthly, As to his being made a *Cardinal*
while at *Come* : this is one of the higheft
pitches and pinacles of Pride (the very next
to the *loftyeft Spire* of the *Pope* himfelf) that
the Romifh Clergy Afpire to, for the *Cardinals* are the *Popes Senatours* or Privy Councellors, and are called *Cardinals*, which is de-
rived from *Cardo*, the *Hinge* of a Door, becaufe upon them (as the Door hangs upon
the Hinge, and turns which way we will,
either for opening or fhutting) all the im-
portant Affairs of the Roman Church hang
and are turned which way they pleafe :
thus the word [*Cardinal*] is ufually ufed
thus,

thus, that whereupon any thing moſt turn-
eth and dependeth, as to *Eaſt, Weſt, North,*
and *South* , are call'd *Cardinal Points of the
Compaſs*.   Thus alſo thoſe *four principal Vertues,* [*Prudence, Juſtice, Fortitude,* and *Tem-*
perance] are call'd the *Cardinal Vertues.* And
thus the Word is *generally* taken to denote
ſomething that is *Chief* and *Principle :* So
theſe *Cardinals* are : But the Hinge, upon
which theſe *Cardinals* did themſelves at the
firſt Hang, was very Low, and their Original Extract very Contemptible : For this
great Office did creep into the *Roman*
Church thus, *Pope Marcellus* in the *Third
Century* divided the City of *Rome* into 25
Pariſhes (ſome Authors call them *Dioceſſes*)
over each of which He appointed a *Presbyter,*
whoſe work was Aſſigned to Baptize Hea-
thens Converted, and to Bury the Dead
within their ſeveral *Precincts* : Theſe were
afterward called *Cardinals* , or *Principal
Prieſts,* or *Deacons,* becauſe they had [*Cu-
ram Animarum*] the Cure of Souls committed to them, and had others (in Sacred
Orders alſo) under them: There be Three
ſorts of *Holy Orders,* ſo called, to diſtin-
guiſh them from their Four other Orders,
(*Door-Keeper, Readers, Exorciſts, Acolyths,*
or *Taper-bearers,*) Theſe are , Firſt, The
Sub-Deacons, (whoſe Office is the Grope-
ing

ing Work, *&c.*) Secondly, The *Deacon*
(who, with the *former*, hath the Honour
only to kiß the Biſhops Hand at the Ordination,) See *Roſſes View*, &c. *pag.* 451.
The Third, Is the *Prieſt*, whom the *Biſhop*
Killeth to ſhew his *Parity* in Reſpect of Order, *Idem Ibidem.* Theſe ſame 25 *Prieſts* of
ſo many Pariſhes in the City, being always
ſo nigh the *Pope*, the more that *he* grew up
gradually into his Grandeur, the higher
did *he* draw up theſe *Prieſts* (his Appurte-
nances) their poſture all along keeping
pace with the *Popes* Pomp, *Adeò ut quod in
principio Oneri fuit; Tandem Aliquandò Hono-
ri eſſe Cæpit.* So, that which at firſt was
but a *Poor* and *Burdenſom* Office, became at
length an Employ of Dignity and Honour :
Thus Dr. *Heylin* Teſtifieth, That *Pope Paſchal*
the *Firſt* cauſed the *Prieſts* of the ſeveral
Pariſhes in *Rome*, by reaſon of *their* nearneſs
to his Perſon, their preſence at his Election,
to be Honoured with a more Venerable
Title, that is, to be called Cardinals, *See
Coſmogr. pag.* 107. at the Top. Thus from
a company of pitiful *Pariſh Prieſts*, they
account themſelves not only Check-Mates
to Princes, but alſo Compeers with Kings
themſelves; but indeed they ought to be
eſteemed the principal Limbs of the *Beaſt
Antichriſt*; yea, they are ſo far Incorpo-
rated

rated with the *Pope* himself, that they muſt
not (forſooth) ſo much as be let Bloud
without his ſpecial Licenſe ; 'tis (no doubt)
for fear leaſt the Head ſhould be ſo concern'd
in theſe his Special Members, as to Die
with them by Sympathy : The Number of
them at their firſt *Roman Conſtitution* (for
want of a *Divine Inſtitution*) were, as is
aforeſaid , *Twenty Five*, which Dr. *Potter*
worthily Obſerves to be the exact Root
Number of Six Hunndred Sixty Six , the
Number of the Beaſt ; but now they are
Multiplied like a Numerous Spawn, into
much more than Double the Number ;
that depends wholy and ſolely at the *Popes*
pleaſure, who can Blow them out of his
Mouth as many as he pleaſeth ; he can
Breath out a *Cardinal* with as much eaſe,
as he Breaths out the Holy Ghoſt ; yea,
for Doing ſome Notable Jobb in Hand, he
can Breath out, or rather Spit out of his
Palat or Pallace, a matter of Sixteen Cardinals at one Spit, as this preſent *Pope* hath
lately done; Oh what an Improving Leap &
Advance hath *he* now made, whereas while
he was but a *Cardinal*, he is then but a *Created Creature* of the *Pope*, but now that He
is become a God Almighty the Pope, he can
be a Creator of his Creatures : *Monſtrum
Horrendam,* &c. Prodigious were his Priviledges,

viledges, (which not *Chrift*, but *Antichrift*,
beftowed upon him while a *Cardinal*,

As Firft, When ever he Rode abroad to
take Frefh Air, His (Sir) Reverence was
fo Glorified (yet not fo much as *Chrift* was
at his Transfiguration) with his Right Reverend *Red Hat*, and *Rich Robes*, that the
Splendor of *Beth* thefe Dazel'd all Specta-
tors Eyes, yea, the very Blaft of his Body
but paffing by, Blew off all their Hats, and
Bore fo hard upon them, as to Blow them
over, and made them fall down to Worfhip
Him, and to ask of Him his Patriarchal
Bleffing, which He rarely beftowed with
that Ingenuity, as He in the Story did,
who in fo doing, faid, [*Si Populus Vult De-*
cipi, Decipiatur.] Light cheap Words make
Fools fain. No doubt but His Shadow, (as
he is now Pope, and *Peters Succeffor*) can
cure as many Difeafes, as that of *Peters* did.
Pope Innocent the *Fourth*, Graced the *Cardi-*
nals with a *Red* (Fools *Cap*, or) *Hat*, by
his Ordinance in the Twelfth *Century*; and
in the Fourteenth, *Pope Pius* the Second Advanced their Splendor yet Higher, with
moft Stately Scarlet Gowns, (Dr. *Heylins*
Cofmogr. pag. 108. *at the bottom.*) Thus
were they Attired in fuch Antick, Gawdy
and Pedantick Dreffes, as neither *Chrift* nor
his *Apoftles* ever Strutted about in, which
muft

muft Declare to all the World, that this is the *Antichrift*, and none need fay of *Him*, as *John Baptift* faid often to Chrift, [*Art thou He that fhould come, or may we look for another?*] No, this is the *Red Letter-Man*, in his *Red Hat* and *Scarlet Gown*. This is the *Bloudy* and *Scarlet Coloured Beaft*.

The Second eminent priviledge this *Cardinal* was dignified with by his Creator the *Pope*, is, that whatever condemned Malefactor (juft going to the place of Execution) could but be fo happy as to meet this Man in his Ponticalibus in the way of his Progrefs, *He* was immediatly to be Acquitted, and his Life fpared, that He might evermore Admire and Adore this his *Romifh Saviour*. 'Tis pitty his clemency is not more exercifed out of defign in this Life-Saving Work : Oh what a choice Act of Mercy might He fometimes do here in but *croffing* the way at a right Juncture, betwixt *Newgate* and *Tyburn*, when his Pontifical Prefence is bleft with fuch an excellent Vertue as both to *fatisfie* the Nations Law, (which is mortally broken) and *Save* alfo the Life and Soul of the condemned.

A Third *Immunity* He had alfo in that *Cardinal Capacity*, was, that no *Cardinal* can be Condemned for the moft Capital Crime, except He can firft be Convicted by the

the Teſtimony of Seventy Two Witneſſes.
By this means, a *Cardinal* may ſafely ven
ture to be the greateſt, *Villain* in the World,
not onely becauſe the Canon-Law ſaith
[*Ecclefia fit libera*] let Church-Men be free
from ſecular Cenſures, but alſo (though the
aforeſaid may fail) if they do but obſerve
their own Jeſuitical Rule [*ſi non caſtè, ta-*
men cautè] He may without hazard perpe-
trate *Whoredom, Treaſon*, the worſt of wick-
edneſs, ſo he do it with caution, and he
deſerves to be hang'd ſeventy two times
over, that will act his Villany in the preſence of ſeventy two perſons, that may all
come in as joynt Witneſſes againſt Him:
The Law of the true and onely wiſe God
(*ſuppoſing* the Teſtimony of *two or three*
Witneſſes ſufficient) is but comparatively
an Inſipid Sentence: but the Law of
their Lord God the Pope is far more
profound, ſaying, two or three and
twenty are not enough of Witneſſes,
even againſt the *Inferiour Clergy*. There
muſt (ſay they) be twenty ſeven a-
gainſt a *Deacon*, ſixty four againſta Prieſt,
and ſeventy two againſt a *Biſhop-Cardinal*.
Dianæ compendium, pag. 85. No wonder if
the Romiſh Clergy be the greateſt Rogues,
and vileſt Villains in the World: No wonder if they carry ſo deep, and ſo Epidemick
　　　　　　　　　　　　　　　　a Tinc-

a Tincture as the only and unparallel'd
Tools to be employed by *Belzebub*, for
Murdering of Kings, *Blowing up of Parliaments*, managing not only Privat and Perſo-
nal Aſſaſinations, but alſo Publick and Na-
tional Maſſacres, to Aſtoniſhment ; to ſay
nothing of Burning down Cities and Mar-
ket-Towns, and many more Matchleſs Miſ-
chiefs, whereof how far this *their Holy Father* (both while *Cardinal*, and when *Pope*)
in Conjunction with his *Unholy Sons* have
been guilty, the Sequel will Demonſtrate ;
and that *Ex abundanti.*

A Fourth *Priviledg* (or rather a Prerogative) this *Cardinal* had, while ſo, was,
That whoſoever would dare to Offend or
Injure (in any kind) his *Worſhip* or *Cardinalſhip*, though the *Offence* were only an
opprobrious Word, and though the *Offen-
der* were ſo *Lofty* as a *King* or an *Emperor*
(who apprehend themſelves above the
comprehenſions of the Law) yet the Popiſh *Canon-Law* Runs thus ſeverely againſt
them, [*Læſæ Majeſtatis Rei Sunt, cujuſ
cunq; ſint Ordinis, Imò Imperator ipſe,* &c.
Et In pænas Bullæ Cænæ Incurrent.] Such
Offenders againſt a *Cardinal* (yea though
it be the *Emperor* himſelf) ſhall be Judged
Guilty of High-Treaſon, and ſhall Incur the
Pains and Penalties of Excommunication, De-

D   . poſition,.

pofition, &c. Was not this a *Lofty Beaft*
then? Exalting himfelf above all that is called God, or *Magiftrates*, even of the very
higheft Form, 2 Thef. 4. 4. He might,
while in *that Capacity* only, challenge the
Stouteft King or Emperor, to affront his
Cardinalfhip, while he ftood thus ftrongly
Guarded by his Canon-Law, to Batter them
down with its Horrible and Terrible Canon-
Bullets; nay, That *Canon-Law* did not
only thus fecure his Perfon, but it alfo ex-
tends to protect his very Houfe, and all
his Hang-bys, or Menial Servants, to all his
Creatures and Favourites in his Prefence;
even all thefe his Appertinances are troubled with that Difeafe called [*Noli me Tan-
gere*] They muft not (forfooth) be *touch-
ed*, though never fo Criminal, 'tis an Affront of the higheft Nature, even *High-
Treafon* it felf, and therefore (with my
confent) fhould any of his *Clerks* be afflicted with the *Kings-Evil* (as they are over-
run with the *Popes-Evil*) a Caveat fhall be
Entred to Debar them of the *Royal-Touch*,
leaft by a Male-Improvement thereof, they
turn their *Canon*-Mouth againft the King:
How, neither the *Cardinal*, nor any of his
Attendants (every one bearing for his Motto, the fame with the Bafe Thiftle, [*Nemo
me Impunè laceffit*,] none can touch me
withouot

without Pricking their own Fingers) ſtand
Fortified with the *Grand* Diabolo's, or Great
Canons of that Canon-Law. See *Dianæ
Compendium, pag.* 93.

The Fifth Prerogative this *Cardinal* had,
above all Kings and Emperors, is, That
whereas *They, Poor Low Shrubs* (in compa-
riſon of ſuch a *Tall Cedar* as a *Cardinal* is)
muſt humble themſelves to the very Foot
of the Pope, muſt Honour the very Shadow of his Shoe-ſtrings, or rather Adore
the *Sparkling* Diamonds, wherewith the
Buckles of his Pantofle is moſt Richly E-
nambled, and the Higheſt Honour that
thoſe *Kings* and *Emperours* muſt have vouch-
ſafed to them, (a Glorious Vouchſafement
and Low Condeſcention in his *Unholineſs*
indeed) is only to Kiſs the Stinking Toe of
his Gowty Gulls : but when this *Cardinal*
came to pay his Viſits, and do his Homage,
unto his Mighty God *Pope Clement* the *Tenth,*
(his immediate Predeceſſor) he had the
Honour (without any proſtrating poſture,
ſave only a *ſlight Congee)* to Kiſs his Ho-
lineſſes Hands, with a Mental Reſervation
too, (Right *Romaniſt* like) wiſhing him
well in his Grave, that he might (upon
ſuch an Irreſiſtible Reſignation) yeild up
his Pontifical Chair to him : Nay, the *Royal
Complement* of *Kiſſing the Popes Hand* only,

was

was not all the Honour he had from him,
but he is allowed to *Kiſs* the *Popes Mouth*
too. *Lorinus* the Jeſuit, in *Aɛt. 6.* doth acknowledg this *Ceremony* (as to matter of
Faɛt) to be the *Cardinals Prerogative* above
Kings and *Emperours :* If the Kiſſing of the
Biſhop by the Prieſt at his Ordination, do
declare a Parity , as above : So this likewiſe muſt be an Indication, that a *Cardinal*
is a *Popes* Fellow, yet Advanced above
Kings and Emperours, (contemptible Titles and Offices to his) by this mutual Em-
bracement. The *Hebrew* Rabbins do Read
theſe words, [*Gnal Pi Jehovah*] *Deut. 34.*
5. which we Tranſlate [*According to the*
Word of the Lord] in this Senſe, That *Mo-*
ſes Died at the Mouth of Jehovah, (which
indeed the *Hebrew* Words do Genuinely and
Gramatically ſighifie,) as if God had taken away *Moſes* his Soul out of his Body
with a Kiſs in a moſt friendly manner :
could this Lord God the *Pope* (*Clement* the
Tenth) have done ſo to *Cardinal Odeſchal-*
cho, when he Kiſs'd him, it had been no better than *Oſculum Iſcarioticum.* rather a Treacherous, than an Amicable Kiſs; in ſpoil-
ing his Market, of deſigning to become his
Succeſſor upon the Papal Throne, and then
had the World wanted him for Pope *Innocent*
the *Eleventh,* though both the Place and the
Title

Title might have been supplied by some o-
ther Person : Had this happen'd so, *That
Pope* might have cry'd Quits for his wishing
(in his Mental Refervation afore mentioned) the Pontifical Chair before the Time :
what loss this might have been to the *Roman*
Church, I know not, but this I know upon
more Infallible proofs than his own. Infallibi-
lity, that had he *Died at the Mouth of his Lord
God the* Pope, when that Complemental Kiss
pass'd betwixt him and his Predecessor, he
had undoubtedly pass'd off the Stage with
less Guilt, the *Horrid Popish Plot*, the Murder of Sir *Edmondbury Godfrey*, and a Thoufand more *Diabolical Intriegues* fince that, will
lay with weight upon some Bodies Conſcience sooner or later. *Veniet , Veniet , qui
malè Judicata Rejudicabit Dies :* There is
a Day coming , which shall Judg Righte-
oufly all Matters over again , (though
at present they be Hush'd up in Judgment) and *this may* be done even in this
World.

I add to all the former the Sixth Priviledg, For so many must be the Number,
that it may the better Symbolize , and
carry a Correspondency with the Number
of the Beasts Name, which confifts of Three
Sixes, [666.] and therefore feveral *Popes*
bore the Number of *Sixtus ,* and had I been

of the Conclave (an Honour I am no way Ambitious of) I would have advised the Cabal, that this *Pope Elect* should have taken upon him no other Name, save that former Name of *Sixtus*, and I would have press'd this Cogent Argument, That seeing there had been before, *Sixtus* the Firſt, the Second, the Third, the Fourth, and the Fifth, now One that will be Stiled *Sixtus* the Sixth, not only makes the *Odd* Number *Even*, but alſo the very Name will carry along with it a moſt Grateful Sound and Symphony : This only would have been the miſchief thereof, that it might have Bordered a little too near the *Number of the Name* of the Apocalyptick Beaſt, for this Name would have conſiſted of *Two Sixes*, (*Sixtus* the Sixth) but that Name conſiſts of *Three* : notwithſtanding this little difference (in an *Unit*) it might have Sounded ſome Alarm to the World : This ſo much neceſſary *Sixth* Priviledg which this Cardinal *Odeſchalcho* had, was, That his Cardinalſhip did Conſtitute him an *Ecclefiaſtick Prince*, whereby he became a fit Mate and Side-Fellow (ſtanding upon equal and even Ground) with the moſt Potent Secular Prince in *Europe*, and therefore to Comport with this Princely Greatneſs, the Canon Law allows him a proportionable

tionable Grandeur, Sumptuous Furniture, and all manner of Pompous Splendor for Supporting the Honour of that Dignity, for to be one of the College of Cardinals is the Penultimate Promotion in the *Roman* Church, it being the very Higheft and Uppermoft Step, from which one or other of thefe Crafty Climbers, Lands at laft into *Peters Chair.* And feeing *Wealth* is an Indifpenfible Perquifite, as it is commonly call'd the *Sinews of War,* fo 'tis no lefs the *Nurfe to Honour,* yea, oft times more than *Vertue,* upon this account, Their Canon Law allows them moft Rich Revenues, moft Rapacious Offices and Employs, wherein (as if they had got the *Philofophers Stone*) they turn all they touch into Gold and Guineys: The *Italian* Author of the *Juft weight of the Scarlet Gown,* gives a Candid and Ingenuous Account, (keeping the Scales *even*) of thofe *Crafty Intrigues,* and many Subtle Tricks, that thofe Arch-Politicians do put in Practice to Enrich themfelves, to fill their Coffers by Sale of Offices that are Vacant, by Penfions from the Court of *Foreign* Princes, (both *France, Spain,* and *Germany*) who all ftrive, not only to Counterballance one another, but alfo, by a pretty *Greafo-Fifto,* with Yellow Ointment to Tilt the Ballance, and fo fome-

times Advance their own Faction uppermoft, through the prevailing Intereft of
thofe their clofely obliged Creatures the
Cardinals, who have fuch a mighty Influence
upon all Debates and Refolves in that
Pragmatick and *Superintendent* Court,
which *Lords* it, and *Laws* it, (or at leaft
would willingly do fo) not only over *Gods*
Herritage the Church, but alfo over the
whole Habitable World.   .

The *Scarlet Gown* Author, in his *Epift.*
Dedic. fpeaks of the feveral Applications
that are made to this Confiftory of Cardinals, from all Popifh *Princes* and States,
efpecially from the Two Mighty Kings of
France and *Spain*, by their Ambaffadors,
who ever lay *Ledger* at that Court, and
who always Addrefs themfelves to the moft
Politick and Powerful of thefe Cardinals,
ftriving to Outvie each other in their proffer
of Fat Penffons to them, giving them the
beft Spiritual Dignities and Promotions
their Two Kingdoms can afford them,
(which in either of them are plentiful
enough) provided always, they will be
engaged thereby to Efpoufe (as much as
ever they may) the Interefts of their Be-
nefactors Crown, to which they are thus
obliged. Herein thefe Court-Penfioners do
Try the Trick of a Treacherous *Judas*,
(who

(who with his [*Quid Dabitis?*] *What will*
ye give me ? and *I will betray my Innocent*
Mafter, &c.) rather than play the part of
Faithful *Peter,* (whofe Succeffors, though
unlike him, fave only in Denying his Lord,
they would be reputed) in Defending his
Innocent Mafter from thofe that Affaulted
him : for notwithftanding never fo ftrong
Engagements and Affurances ; Oh what a
flippery Hold either or both thofe great
Princes have of thefe their *Cardinal* Engines, who frequently (and upon very
flight occafions) are found to warp into
the contrary Faction, which Verifies the
Vulgat Proverb, *'Tis Hard to make a Faft*
Bargain with a Loofe Chapman : They however, in playing thus at *Faft* and *Loofe* can
notably ferve their own Ends , and like
Bad Lawyers can take a Bribe upon both
Sides, when they are Courted by both the
Kings. Efpecially thofe Cardinals that fit
neareft the Papal Chair, and are in the
faireft Capacity to Climb next into it, as
was the Happy Cafe of this our Cardinal,
and therefore muft be Highly Courted by
Foreign Agents in the Name of their Mafters ; The Height of whofe Ambition it
was to oblige him. Thus we fee this *Bene-*
detto Odefchalcho had fair opportunities for
gaining Wealth enough to maintain his
　　　　　　　　　　　　　　　Grandeur;

Grandeur, the Canon-Law doth Command thefe Cardinals, that, befides their Living upon the Churches Revenues, to catch what they can for themfelves, .(may we Add, *Per Fas & Nefas* , *Vel Vi* , *Vel Clam* , *Vel Precariò*, either by Hook or Crook, to wit, the Crofier Statf,) upon the Account of Aggrandizing the *Roman* Clergy, which Poverty would render Contemptible, *Dianæ Compendium*, pag. 88.

How far this Cardinal comply'd (as who of that Cathólick Faith would not) with that Canon-command , we fhall have an Account By and By : But before we can come to that, Here are Two mifchievous Stumbling-ftones lays in our Way like aCouple of Blockado's, which who ever were able to Roll away out of our Way, would do us a very great Kindnefs ; when fet faft.

The *Firft* is this, Suppófe this Cardinal had been a *Monk*, 'tis not to fuppofe what ought not to be fuppofed; for fome *Benedicts* (as his Fore-Name and fome Popes Name were) had been *Benedictine* Monks, and at their entrance into their Monafteries had folemnly vowed *perpetual Poverty* ; how could this Monkifh Man with a good Confcience Relinquifh his *vowed Poverty* ? Gather Riches fo faft that he got the *Devil and all*, (as will appear afterwards) became an

Ecclefi-

Ecclefiaftick Prince, Ride his Progrefs in all Prince-like Equipage, never proud *Haman* more Highly Honoured, and never any Triumphant *Cæfar* or Conquerour better Arrayed than He in his Richeſt Robes for Splendour and Glory : Let any Man come, forth and tell me the Confiſtency of theſe two Contraries, *& erit mihi magnus Apollo.* He that can rightly Reconcile them, ſhall be my Oracle.

Tuſh (faith the Romiſh Cafuiſts, one of the New *Quacks* the *Jefuits*) I can with a wet Finger make theſe two Contraries Jump friendly into one, *two odds* make *even* (as Two odd Threes make even Six, *ſtill he will harp upon the Number Six*, as above) and why may not *two at odds* meet in *even* alſo. This is the Learned Gloſs of the Popiſh Cafuiſts upon this Caſe of Con-ſcience in the *General*, but more particular-ly (he faith) this *Vow of Poverty* was taken with a mental Refervation, that he refolved to be poor, no longer, than while he could not poſſibly be Rich, and ſo the word [*Per-petual*] in the Vow muſt be *vox æquivoca*, and to be taken with equivocation, *&c.*

Such Dirt-Dawbers (that *Dawb with un-temper'd Morter*) are the Jeſuitical Cafuiſts, yea, many *Monks* can play the pranks of a *Monkey* (there is not much difference be-twixt

twixt their Names) who can flip his Collar on *for his Masters Pleasure*, and with as much eafe, can flip it off again *for his own*, The *Monk* can play at faft and loofe with his *strict Vow* as well as the *Monkey* with his *strait Collar.* But above all Cafuifts that fpeak home to this Cafe, hear what an Infallible Pope (*papa in Cathedrâ non poteſt errare*) and that *Innocent* the 10th, (one of the laft before this) fpeaketh ; He furely, cannot fpeak but like a moft profound Oracle : I have heard fome Judicious Clients fay, when I want Councel, I will go to the *Head*, and not to the *Tail*, meaning, to the profoundeft Councellors at Law, and not to the mean, pittiful, underling Lawyers : let us do fo here, omitting all other fcribling puny Cafuifts in *Popiſh Schools* , and hear what this great Oracle faith out of *Peters unerring Chair :* This *Pope Innocent* the Tenth, when he was but Cardinal *Pamphilio*, made a promife in the Conclave to Marry his onely Nephew into the Family of the *Barberinos* (one of the three grand pontifical Factions, *Paulino* and *Pamphilian* being the other two, in that Sacred Colledge or Confiftory) the fame Promife he privatly made to his Nephew alfo ; howbeit, he foon chang'd his mind (being then not in the Papal Chair and fo, nor Infallible) and promoted

moted Him to a Scarlet Gown (inſtead of
a Wife), which was far better, and which
(he thought) would beſt prevent divers
Emergent Differencies that were likely to
ariſe by Marrying one of the *Pamphilian*
Family to a Wife of the *Barberinos*, a contrary Faction, which yet had been wheadled into a Beleif of this great Match for
their She-Cozen, becauſe it was ſo ſolemh-
ly and publickly promiſed by the Cardinal
(the Unkle of the Gentleman, or in plainer Terms, the Father of the Baſtard) in
their Sacred Colledge of Cardinals, where
there was a dead weight of Living Witneſſes
thereof. Notwithſtanding this *Promiſe*, a
Sacred thing in it ſelf, made in a Sacred
place, and before ſo many ſacred Perſons
(according to Popiſh Sentiments) he made
a ſhift to *cozen* both *them* and their *She-Co-*
zen : whereupon, not long after His Af-
ſumption into the Papal Chair (no doubt
but his Nephew in his new Scarlet Gown,
gave his Uncle an heaty lift thither) Cardinal *Antonio Barberinos,* having ſtill the grum-
bling of his Gizzard for the late cheating
affront, makes his Addreſs to his New-Cre-
ated and Now-Crowned *Holineſs* (expect-
ing nothing but what was Holy Redreſſes
ſuitable to his new Title, to ſweeten unto all
his new Crown and Dignity) He therefore
brake

brake out into thofe words to this new Pope
Innocent the 10*th.* (into which he had changed his Name *Pamphylio*) faying, *Moſt Bleſ-
fed Father, your Tranſactions about your Nephew* (*in Marrying him to a Scarlet Gown,
and not to our Cozen*) *doth not well correſpond
with your promiſes made to us in the Conclave,
when you was but Cardinal :* Hereupon his
new *Un-Holineſs* (with a great deal of Gravity, as became his Place) as Un-Holily Anfwered, thus faying, *Tell me my Lord, who
was He, that made ſuch promiſes to you ? Was
it not Cardinal Pamphilio ?* Yes, faith *Antonio,* upon which the Pope turns fhort upon
him, and bids him go challeng his Promife
of *Pamphilio*, for he was not the Man of
that Name now, His Name was *Innocent*
the *Tenth,* and not that Man you Imagine
me to be : At this, *Antonio* Raged, and like
a new *Mongi Bello,* Fire ſtarted out of his
Eyes, and like Old *Orlando,* ſtamps with his
Feet upon the Ground, when he heard the
Infallible Chair fpeak more Fallibly and
Fallacioufly, than ever the Devil did at his
Delphos-Oracle : In this Tranſport his
Voice alfo Vomited out fome fevere Inve-
ctives againſt his Lord God the Pope, and
in an High Difguſt, Uncivilly turns his Tail
upon his Blafphemed , as well as Blaf-
pheming Idol , Excommunicates himfelf
from

from the *Sacred Consistory*, and from the Metrapolitan City of *Rome* (the very place of his own Nativity) flies into *France* to be Protected by the *French* King, at whose Devotion he had all along been in the Faction, leaving all his Riches (he had Vastly scraped together) and Revenues behind him : See the Substance of this whole Story in the Author of the *Just Weight of the Scarlet Gown*, his own *Preface* to his Book; who tells us likewise, *pag.* 68. That this *Don Antonio Barberino* (who thus Dif-resented this profound, more than *Jesuitical*, the Diabolical Salvo of his Holy Father) was none of the Best, who kept for his Miss or Whore, *La Checa Bufona*, upon whom he wasted most Vast Sums of Money, *&c. pag.* 69.

Mark here, This Papal *Distinction* without a Difference (to wit, it was not *Innocent* the Pope, but *Pamphilio* the Cardinal, that made the Promise, and therefore not at all obliging, *&c.*) is the Best Bramble-Bush, that the Infallible Chair it self can find out, wherewith to stop the Gap in a *Romish* Conscience ; and if this will serve as a sufficient Salvo for the Supreme Pope himself, much more for his Underling, a *Cardinal* ; and so our *Odeschalcho* is brought off with flying Colours ; It was not *Odes-*

chalcho

chalcho the *Cardinal* that *Vowed perpetual Poverty*, it was only *Odeſchalcho* the *Monk* that did ſo, I am not He that made that Vow, 'tis not obliging to me, as a *Cardinal*, but leaſt of all, as now I am *Pope*.

Such ſlippery Tricks of the *Monkey*, we find the *Jeſuits* can play, as well as the *Monks*; for *Caſimer* the *Jeſuit* could (by his Fervent Prayers to his Founder *Ignatius Loyola*) obtain an effectual Diſpenſation for his Acquitment from his *Holy Orders* to Embrace a Crown, the Jewels whereof had a Sovereign Vertue to Salve all Wounds of Conſcience, and to give him a *Quietus Eſt* : Hereupon he became the *King* of *Poland :* but while I think of it, Take this pleaſant Story, I have ſometimes Read with complacency, 'tis this, The Biſhop of *Triers* (I think, but am ſure it was one of thoſe Biſhops that are the *Electoral Princes* of the *Emperour* of *Germany*) was found fault with for ſome Notorious Extravagances in his Publick Miniſtrations, by a very *Grave Senator*, Who told him, Such Groſs Actings were a Scandal to his Lawn Sleeves and Mitre ; all the Apology that Proud *Prelate* could make for himſelf, was this, He Anſwered, That he did not thoſe things as he was a *Biſhop*, but as he was a *Prince :* But the *Senator* Replies in a cutting Reprimend, ſaying,

saying, *If the Devil get the Prince for such Crimes, I pray you, what will become of the Bishop.* This Non-plus did not admit of a Rejoinder; and is there not *par Ratio* in both these Cases of Conscience aforementioned, If the Devil get *Pamphilio* the Cardinal for breaking his Promise, (contrary to *Psal.* 15.) what will become of *Innocent* the *Pope* ; it may be, he hath got them *Both* together at one Mouthful (being but one Individual Man) already, seeing Pope *Innocent* the *Tenth*, who was before, *Cardinal Pamphilio*, is now Trip'd off the Stage, and our *Odeschalcho* is got into the Chair in his Room : So likewise, If the Devil get the *Monk* for breaking his *Vow of perpetual Poverty*, what will become of the *Rich Cardinal*, sure I am, Though the Devil hath not already made one Mouthful of them both, yet, the *Pope* (the Devils Eldest Son) hath done it, for both *Odeschalcho* the *Monk* (as some say) and *Odeschalcho* the *Cardinal* are at once Swallowed up by this present Pope, *Innocent* the *Eleventh*.

The Upshot of the whole in a word is this, I Refer to the Judicious Reader, whether this *Grave Senator*, or the Jesuits (*Azorius, Navar,* &c.) yea the *Infallible Chair* it self, be the better *Casuist* ; and whether *Don Antonio Barberino*, the *Crook-Back*

E   Nephew

Nephew to Pope *Urban*'the *Eighth*, were not a *Straighter* Man of the Two, that Abhor'd thofe wicked Evafions of Pope *Innocent* the *Tenth*, as above.

- But having well wearied both my *Self* and my *Reader*, with lifting at this great *Stone* that lay in our Way, and yet cannot get it Removed out of the Way half fo well as was *Amafa*'s Stab'd Body, that ftop'd the *March* of the Army, 2 *Sam.* 20. 12. 'Tis high time to leave it, and to try our Strength in a Lift or Two at the *Second*, which in like manner obftructs our paffage, in giving a particular Character of this *prefent Pope*.

The *Second Objection* is, Whether thefe pretended Governors of the Church, the Popifh *Prelates* and *Cardinals*, abounding in all manner of *Pride*, *Pomp* and *Luxury*, can by any fober Mind be Deemed the *Rightful* Succeffors of *Chrift* and his *Apoftles*, who all did fo oft Recommend *Self-Denyal* and *Humility*, &c.

To this, in fhort, I fhall Anfwer, with a Story that I have Read many Years ago, and which I have lately met with in the *Hiftory of Cardinals*, pag. 46. The Author of *Nipotifmo di Roma*, (wherein he fhews how Sedulous every Pope is to promote his Nephews or Baftards) Relates the *Matter of*

Fact

Fact thus, being both an *Eye* and an *Ear-*
Witnefs thereof in Perfon himfelf, faying,
I Remember a certain Sermon I heard in a
Covent in *Rome*, and in the prefence of
Two *Cardinals*, (it may be our *Odefchalcho*
was one of them) and Cardinal *Sacchetti*
was the other ; The Preacher was a *Bare
Footed Francifcan*, who feem'd a poor pitiful
Creature to look upon, yet geting into the
Pulpit (on the firft *Sunday* in *Lent*) in a
very great Auditory, after an *Ave-Maria*,
and Two or Three Cringes (as is ufual)
with his Knee, rifing up again upon his
Feet, and pulling his Cappuce or Cowle
upon his Head, down almoft over his Eyes,
he paufed a while (in this pofture) without fpeaking a word, and fixing his Eyes
ftedfaftly upon the *Cardinals* that ftood before him, without Naming any Text at all,
ie breaks out abruptly into thefe words,
St. Peter *was a* Fool, St. Paul *was a* Fool,
ill the *Apoftles were Fools*, all *the Holy Mar-
yrs*, all the *Primitive Saints of the Church of
Jefus Chrift our Redeemer, were Fools.*]
The *Cardinals* were ftrangely Stun'd with
hefe words, and ftood as Infenfible as Two
tatues; the People alfo, and I among the
eft, Admiring this unufual Freak, were
ontent enough to Attend the Attendency
f it : The *Fryar*, after fome fmall filence

(which he purpofely did, to obferve the Refentments of his Auditory) began his Difcourfe as followeth, [*You that are Pre-lates, do not you believe, you fhall be Saved?* I know your Anfwer, *Yes*, Father *Fryar*, *we do. And you People, you are certain of Pa-radife?* without Doubt, you will fay, *Yes* too. *Yes*, faith the *Fryar*, What, will Turning Night into Day, by Feafting, Sporting and Luxury? Will Frequenting Play-Houfes, Whore-Houfes, and a Living in all manner of Debauchery, bring *you* [*People*] to Heaven?

As for *you* [*Prelates,*] Will your Wear-ing *Purple* aad *Scarlet*, Will your Glittering in Gold and Silver, Will your Riding a-broad, and Carreeceing about in Gawdy Coaches, and when you come out of them, Will the having your Silken Trains carry'd after you in the Street, bring you to Hea-ven? Will your Spoiling the Walls of the *Church*, to Adorn the Walls of your *Cham-bers*, and will your Subtrafting from *Chrift*, to beftow upon the World, bring you thi-thither? Would you Oh *Romaniffs*, be Saved in this manner? Is this the *way to Salvation? which* we are told is not a *Broad* but a *Narrow Way*.

Then certainly all the *Apoftles*, and all the *Saints of the Primitive Church* might have

have been Saved in the fame Way, as well as you ; and then as certainly they were all *Mad Men* and *Fools*, to *Wander up and down in Sheep Skins*, and *Goat Skins*, being *Deftitute*, and *Afflicted*, to Undergo the *Hard Tryals of Cruel Mockings and Scourgings*, yea, *moreover of Bonds and Imprifonments*, yet higher, they were *Mad Men* and *Fools* to *be Stoned*, to be *Sawn Afunder*, to be *Slain with the Sword*, and to be *Tortured* and *Tormented* , not *Accepting Deliverance* , &c. *Heb.* 11. 35, 36, 37, 38. If *your Way* be the Way to Heaven.

But the miftake is on your part, Oh *Romanifts*, They were all *prudent* and *pious Men*, , 'Tis *You* that are the *Madmen* and *Fools*, and not *They*. 'Tis *You* that propofe a new way of Salvation to your Selves, which will beft comport with your own Vanity and Villany, even fuch a way, as is not onely contrary to the Holy Gofpel, but to the very light of *Right Reafon* alfo.

This fingle ftory is fufficient of it felf, to Demonftrate what kind of Succeffours thefe *Cardinals* (and amongft the reft our *Odefchalcho*) are to the *Apoftles*, The *pattern* and the *portraiture* do correfpond like *Harp* and *Harrow* ; which made the *Italian Painter* Draw the Pictures of *Peter* and *Paul*, with a very deep Tincture of a Red Vermilion

E 3 Colour

Colour in both their Complexions, and when fome *Cardinals* blamed him for putting an Abufe upon their holy Predecefíours (to Limn them more like *Good Fellows*, who had been taking a Cup of N*ims*, a little too much of the comforting. Creature) He Smartly yet Modeftly Anfwered, No, Gentlemen, you miftake my Genuine meaning, for there you may behold thofe two *Holy Apoftles* no other than *Blufhing* at *you* their fuch *Unholy Succeffours*.

I fhall conclude this Paragraph with that ftrange Prayer of a *Proteftant Divine* upon his Reading a *Gazet*, who there found, how in the Vacancy of the *Roman* See, fome Cardinals were confulting, that the next Pope when Created, fhould be bound to difcard his *Nephews*, thofe *Suckers of the Churches Treafure.* He Zealoufly Ejaculated this fhort, but pithy, Petition, faying, [*God Almighty Remove thefe good Thoughts out of the Minds of thefe Cardinals*, for the *Scandal of their Church*, are the *Edification of ours*, and Difturbances amongft them, gives a Sweet Repofe to us : *Hiftory of Cardinals*, pag. 132.

Suitable to that before, is this, that which followeth after. Another *Divine* Difcourfing with Cardinal *Odefchalcho's* Chaplain, and asking him what he was, he Anfwered, *I*
am

am a Priest, and pray you, faith the Mini-
ster, what is your Master whom you Serve,
Oh Sir (quoth he) 'tis my *Lord Cardinal*:
Go to then, said the Enquirer, pray what
is your Work ? Oh *Sir* (faith he) *I Say*
Service in my Lords Chappel ; *Say Service,*
(faith the other) then you are not so good
as an *Horse* or an *Asse,* for both these dumb
Creatures *doe Service,* and *doing Service* is
better than *Saying Service* : but the Discourse
ended not here, the *Opponent,* a little too
Pragmatical, must ask some more Questi-
ons, being too much Question-sick, fur-
ther, saying, I pray you Sir, who gave to
you the Name of *Priest,* and to your Master the Name of *Lord Cardinal,* seeing St.
Paul Names no such Offices among the
Officers of the True Church ? *Ephes.* 4. 11.
The *Respondent* Replys, Oh Sir, Our *Holy*
Mother the Church gave to me the Name of
Priest, and to my Master the Name of *Car-*
dinal. Upon this, the *Questionist* makes this
brisk Repartee, saying, [God Almighty
Bless me with my *Fathers* Name, for all that
Bear only their *Mothers* Name, (as you
say, *You* and your *Lord* do) be no better
than *Bastards,* or if you will have it in a
cleaner Dress, that is to say, the *Popes Ne-*
phews : But enough of this *Facetious Dis-*
course..

E 4　　　　Now

Now 'tis High time to take a more particular View of our *Odefchalcho*, whom we have Characteriz'd but little as a *Cardinal* hitherto, feeing our main *Defign is, to give him a more Ample Character as *Pope*, where the *Myftery of Iniquity* muft be more fully opened in a large Field of Difcourfe.

As *Fobn* the *Divine* gives a Graphical Defcription of the Picture of his *Double Beaft in general*; how *He* gradually Rofe, both out of the *Earth*, and out of the *Sea*, *Revel.* 13. 1, 11. So my prefent Task is to Limn to the Life the very Perfon of this prefent *Scarlet Colour'd Beaft*, the *Pope* in particular, fhewing, *Firft*, How he rofe up Step by Step to the *Pontifical Chair*, into which this our Cardinal *Odefchalcho* was Ufher'd with abundance of Pompous and Solemn *Ceremonies* : 'Tis indeed an ufual Saying, That *Ceremonies* are but *Indifferent things*; yet this is a moft certain and Tryed Truth, (to the great Detriment of many, much Damnified hereby) that though *Ceremonies* be in truth but things *Indifferent* to *Salvation*, yet Experience (the beft School-Miftrefs) Teacheth, they are things *Neceffary* to *Preferment*. None can Climb up (not *Jacob's*, but) *Antichrift's* Ladder, fave fuch as have the *Cheveril* Confcience of

a *Latitu-*

a *Latitudinarian*, who can ſtretch out and
Gape wide as the Greedy-gut once did,
(in his Eating a Fiſh Dinner) who ſwal-
lowed down Bones and all, till he had like
to have been Choaked : We muſt ſuppoſe
our *Odeſchalcho* had a Throat wide enough,
he was not at all ſo *Scrupulous* as the *precife*
Ones among us, but could Gulp down any
Romiſh Ceremony (though never ſo Corrupt
and Unſcriptural) provided it might but
give him an Hearty Lift into the *Seat of In-*
fallibility : 'Tis as much beyond Queſtion-
ing, as the moſt Received *Maxim* in Phylo-
ſophy, That ſuch as are moſt *Defective* in
their *Morals*, are moſt Zealous to ſupply
it with *abundance* of *Ceremonials* : How far
this our *Odeſchalcho* was *Deficient* in *Mora-*
lity, let the Author of the *Scarlet Gown*
(his own Countrey-man, the *Italian*) be
heard to ſpeak , His Relation Runs thus,
Benedetto Odeſchalcho was a very *Rich Pre-*
late, who a long time Courted *Don Barbe-*
rino for preferring him to be *Clerk* of the
Chamber, which place he was Ambitious of,
(that he might be the better Acquainted
with all the Grand Intrigues of the Confi-
ſtory) and which the *Don* had promiſed
him upon his paying down upon the Nail
a Round Sum of Money for it : But finding that his Purchaſe proved nothing, ſave
only

only a company of Court Complements, and that this *Crooked-back Don Antonio* dealt but *Crookedly* with him, in making the Fool fain with Fair Words without Deeds, he (being weary'd with a little fprinkling of Court Holy Water only,) began to think of the Proverb too late, *That a Fool and his Money is foon parted* : He hereupon Refolves to take new Meafures, and to try whether (againft, and to Confute all *Gramer* Rules,) the *Fæminine Gender* might not prove more Worthy than the *Mafculine*, and whether the *Gray-Mare* might not prove the better *Horfe* ; fo makes he his Application to that Famous Strumpet, that Imperious *Jezabel*, Sifter in Law, *&c.* to Pope *Innocent* the *Tenth*, *Don Olympia*, wherein 'tis Remarkable, that he deals in both with the *Dons*, and with the Greateft *Dons* too, the one an Ambitious, and (as to the Court Faction in *Rome*) a very *Potent Cardinal* ; but the other (when he fhifts his Sails unto, and makes his *Second* fhift) was no lefs than an Omnipotent Creatrefs ; for fhe could Create what *Cardinals* and what *Pepes* fhe pleafed, with her Irrefiftible Charms : No wonder then, if, when at a lofs, he falls upon this new Expedient, and Turns *Don Antonio* into *Don Olympia* , yea Turns from the former to the latter , as being better

furnifhed

furnished with Conveniences for him : he now thought it nothing so Commodious to *Court a Lord*, as to *Court a Lady*, especially One so Accomplished both with an Almighty Power , and with a Bewitching Beauty.

Et si qua latent, Meliora putat, Ovid.

Was not this a Brisk Madam , and well worth a Prelate, yea a Cardinals Courting : The Substance of this Account , (though here dress'd up in other Language) may be seen in the *Scarlet Gown* Author, *pag.* 21. who says further , That this *Benedetto* Presented this Lady with Rich Love-Tokens, wherewith at length he *Got into Her*————Favor : But above all (faith the said *Italian*) with One Amourous Bribe more than Ordinary, and most to be Remarked ; which matter (as that Author Relates it) was manag'd after this manner, Our *Odescalcho*, going one Day (as he did often) to pay his Respects to this his Lady *Don Olympia*, about the Coronation of her Brother in Law *Pope Innocent* the *Tenth*, a Goldsmith came at that very time , and shewed *Her* a very fair Cupboard of Rich and Modish Plate to Sell , and perhaps prompting the Lady to Buy it, as conducing

ducing much to the Grace and Honour of
that Great Days Solemnity : *Olympia*
Vieweth it thorough and thorough in the
prefence of this *Odefchalcho* (Her Para-
mour) and other Lords, and no doubt
had more than a Months Mind to it, but
how to compafs it without her own Coft
and Coin, was her prefent Project, in order to this, She firft highly commends every Veffel by it felf, both Mettal, Workman-
fhip and Luftre, and then all in the whole,
faying, It was a goodly and curious Cupboard of the New Fafhion'd Plate, but fhe
was a *Poor Widow* (fhe fhould have faid, a
Rich Harlot) fo pretending fhe was not
able to Purchafe it ; laftly, upon this fhe
withdraws immediately to her Chamber,
leaving the By-ftander *Odefchalcho* (who
admired all for her fake) to make out fome
better proof (than yet he had done in all
his former Gifts) of his Cordial Affections
to Her. This *Prelate* , being but (as the
fame Author calls him) a *Man of mean*
Undeftanding, was the more eafily Infnared
with the wily Wit of a Woman, which, at
a pinch, doth ufually exceed that of a
Man (who Requires more Deliberation)
even of fuch as have deeper Reaches and
Capacities than our fhallow *Odefchalcho* :
Hereupon, under this fuddain Surprize, he
calls

calls the Goldfmith to him, Asks the Price of
the Plate, 'twas below his Honour in his
Amorous Expectations to bid him lower
than was Asked, he paid down Eight Thoufand Crowns for it, and without more Adoe,
fent it in to the Lady , as a Prefent from
Him, to her in her Chamber, that this *Gift*
(as *Solomon* faith) might make Room for
himfelf thither alfo : *Don Olympia* was fo
Tranfported (both with the Succefs of her
Craft, and with the Poffeffion of fo much
Plate, all cofting her Nothing, fave only
Cafting a Figure about a Credulous Fool,)
that Immediately fhe went to the Pope
where fhe was *Domina*, *Fac totum*, and whe-
ther fhe had free Accefs Night and Day,
See *Scarlet Gown*, pag. 81. *at the bottom.*)
Begs of him for *Odefchalcho*, not only the
Clerkfhip in the Chamber, but foon after a
Scarlet Gown alfo . How far this *She-Don*
Help'd him with her Hand (if not in Perfon, yet by Proxy) into *Peters* Chair, I
know not, 'tis enough to know here that
Odefchalcho's Familiar Converfe with this
Famous Woman , but Infamous Whore,
gives Ground enough to beleive, that *He*
was *Defective in Morals*, and therefore was
under a Neceffity to *Eeek* that out *with Ceremonials* : No wonder then, if fuch a Man
of *Immorality* fhould become (as it were) a
very

very Compound of *Ceremony* : His *Election*
to the Chair *confifted of Ceremony* ; his *Coronation* in the Chair *confifted of Ceremony* ;
but above all, his whole Worſhip and Devotion in the matters of Religion *confifteth of
Ceremony* ; only a Word or Two as a By-
blow upon this laſt, it being befide the
Scope of our prefent Defign. This prefent
Popes Worſhip is drawn forth in ſuch an
Antick and *Pedantick* Dreſs, ſo far from the
Simplicity of the Goſpel, that no thinking
Mind can look upon *Popery* to be any better
than *Foppery*, ſure I am, the *Romiſh* Church
is far paſt her *Meridian* , ſeeing ſhe can
ſcarce be now. ſeen for the length of her
own Shadow, the *Shadows of her Evening*
are ſtretched out, in turning *Doctrine* into
Sophiſtry, and *Difcipline* into *Ceremony*, and
though the *Hedg of her Ceremonies* may fa-
vourably *protect Carrion-Crows* , yet is it
pricking and *Vexaticus enough to harmlefs
Doves.*

　　But to Wave that in this place, and come
to that Compound of Ceremonies, manag'd
by a *Mafter of Ceremonies*, at the *Election*
of this prefent *Pope* : No ſooner was his
Predeceſſor, *Pope Clement* the *Tenth* Dead,
(for though the Keys of *Heaven, Hell* and
Purgatory, hang at the Popes Girdle, yet
there's the Miſchief, the Key of the *Grave*
was

was by fome Mifhap or other drop'd from
it, otherwife the Pope had been equally as
Immortal as *Infallible*,) but the Congregation of Cardinals '(having Nine Mornings
after *his* Death Sung Dirges for the Repofe
of his Soul, and preparing themfelves with
Holy Water, Incenfe, *&c.*) did all Repair
to the Conclave, and with them Two Mafters of Ceremonies, and the *Secratary* of
the College, *&c..* were all clofe fhut up together, in order to Elect a New Pope:
Then Proceffions came Thick and Threefold from all Churches and Monafteries,
Singing, [*Veni Creator*, &c. Come Holy
Ghoft, *&c.*] Round about the Conliftory,
Imploring the Infpirations of the Spirit to
come upon the Cardinals: The firft Step or
Ceremony, was, The Three chief Cardinals of the feveral Orders, with the Cardi-
nal-Chamberlain, took an Exact Survey of
all the parts of the Conclave to fee that all
be clofe, and fhut up on all fides, as if
they would fhut out the Holy Ghoft from
coming among them ; for upon the Death
of Pope *Clement* the *Fourth*, when the Conclave could not agree (being divided and
Rent in pieces by the Feuds and Factions of
the *French* and *Spanifh* Intereft) about the
Election of a Succeffor, one of the Cardinals (perhaps fuppofing that they were
too

too clofe fhut up in the Conclave,) cryed,
You muft Order the Uncovering of the Roof of
the Confiftory, to make way for the Holy Ghoft
to come down upon us : The Conclave puts fo
much ftrefs upon this fame *Ceremony*, that
not ftrictly to obferve it, is a Nullity of the
Election.

The *Second Ceremony* at the Election of
this Pope, was, The Mafter of the Ceremonies, (after a Recital of the Cardinals Priviledges, which each Swore to Obferve, in cafe he were chofen Pope,) Rings
a Bell and calls them all to Mafs, at which
they Sang the Hymn, [*Veni Creator Spiri-*
tus,] and the Prayer of the Holy Ghoft,
to Implore His Illumination upon them :
But I am afraid they could not find one
Promife to ground their *Prayer* upon, for
the promife of the Spirits coming is only to
thofe that Seek him *in Spirit and in Truth*,
and that are found *in Due Order*, and not
in fuch Diforders as Ufually attend the Conclave, which once gave occafion to an Old
Cardinal of *Sicily*, (who, after long Ab-
fence, coming to a Popes Election , and
finding nothing but Animofities, Factions
and Fractions among them,) to complain,
faying, *Num ad Hunc Modum fiunt pontifices*
Romani? &c. I expected that fervent
Prayers, as in Times of Old, fhould have
procured

procured fome fit Man to be pointed out
by the Holy Ghoft to us for a *Vicar of*
Chrift, but (faith he) If promifing Re-
wards for Penfionary Votes, If Cajoling,
Curfing and Threatning Revenge b 3 your
way of Canvafing your Elections, then
farwel for me, and fo the good Old Män
Returned Home to his Countrey, and
could never be perfwaded to fee *Rome* any
more.

The *Third Ceremony*, was, To Elect a
Pope by *Scrutiny*, (waving the Two other
ways of *Infpiration* or *Compromife*,) which
they thus managed, Each Cardinal hath a
Lift of all the Cardinals Names given to
him, he Wrote down in a peice of Paper,
whom he would have chofen, went to the
Altar, puts his Scroll into the Golden Cha-
lice ftanding thereupon, and fo Return'd to
his place, when all had fo done, the *Prime*
Bifhop took out all the Papers, delivered
them to the *Prime Deacon*, who unfolded
them all, and without mentioning the *Ele-*
ctor, Read aloud the Names of the *Elected* :
The *Prime Prieft* Reckoning the Voices,
pronounced the *Majority* of Votes to fall
upon *Cardinal Odefchalcho* : Hereupon he
Rang a Silver Bell, and a Pan of Coals was
brought in, and all the Paper Billets, wherein the Names of all the Cardinals were
Written, were Burnt.   F   *Good*

Good God, How far the Ancient Chur&h of *Rome* is now Run from the Primitive Pattern? How far is that Church at this Day Run a Whoring? more like *Babylons Whore*, than *Sions Spouſe*, who both Ask'd and Received Directions from the Bleſſed Bridegroom, how ſhe might follow the Footſteps of *Chriſts* (not *Antichriſts*) Flock: I would gladly Ask of any Man, how many of theſe (and many more, for Brevity, omitted) ſilly *Apiſh* as well as *Popiſh Tricks* and *Trinkets*, were put into practice at the Election of St. *Matthias* into Traiterous *Judas*'s Biſhoprick and *Apoſtleſhip*, Act. 1. 20. to 26. The pure Simplicity of that Primitive Ordination makes our Pope *Innocent* the *Eleventh* look more like an *Unholy Apoſtate*, than any *Holy Apoſtle*, whoſe *Succeſſor* he yet preſumes to be Reckoned, who in Truth is rather a *Succeſſor* of *Judas* in betraying *Chriſt*, as he is the *Antichriſt*, than any of the Holy *Apoſtles*, who were fervent follow-ers of the Sacred Footſteps of their Sweet Saviour, and who Commands us *to follow them no farther*, *than they follow Chriſt*, I Cor. II. I. They make that *Holy Child Jeſus* the *Regula Regulans*, or Rule Ruling, and themſelves only the *Regula Regulata*, the *Rule Ruled*, they would not have us to follow the Dark Side of the *Cloud* of Wit-neſſes,

neſſes, as the *Ægyptians* did, and were
Drowned, but the White-ſide thereof, as
the *Iſraelites* did, and were Saved. Neither do we ever find that St. *Peter* paſs'd
under thoſe Comick and Theatrical Ceremonies when called to his Apoſtleſhip, or
ever ſo Prefer'd or Enrich'd any of his *Nephews* or Baſtards; as the *Pope* (his pretended Succeſſor) doth now.

The *Fourth Ceremony* wherewith this preſent Pope had his Pompous Inauguration at
his Election, was, Still more like *Apoſtati-
cal*, than *Apoſtolical*, to wit; No ſooner was
the Majority of Votes (even Two parts of
Three) acknowledged to fall upon our
Cardinal *Odeſchalcho*, through the Almighty
Influence of his Old *Grateful* as well as
Humble Servant, *Don Olympia*, who could
not, with either *Honour* or *Advantage*, ſo
ſoon forget her Stately Cupboard of curious Silver Plate, well knowing, her laſting
Gratitude to Him would be an Encourage-
ment to others in that Court, to make their
Addreſſes in the ſame manner to Her. No
ſooner (I ſay) was this *Odeſchalcho* owned
to be the *Pope Elect* Duely, though never ſo
Factiouſly and Surreptitiouſly ; but preſently the *Wicket*, or rather *Wicked* Hole
(well call'd the *Golden Door*, through which
the Hungry Cardinals Receive. all their

Meat, as well as *Air*, during their, fometimes, long Confinement,) was then broken open, at which ftood an Infinite Number of Poor People ; on whom this New
Pope beftowed his Papal Benediction, and
to whom He Remitted all their Sins . The
Formality of opening this *Golden Door*, was
thus Obferved, This New Pope came with
a *Golden Mallet* in his Hand (all *He* med-
dles now with muft be Gold,) His *Silver
Age* is now turned into a *Golden* One, his
Silver Cupboard of Plate before purchafed,
is now turned into a *Golden Door*, and into
a *Golden Mallet*, yea, better than all this.
Here was, by Vertue of the Philofophers
Stone, a *Silver*, or rather a *Leaden*, or *Cop-
per Cardinal* (as *Odefchalcho* fignifies) into
a more Illuftrious and *Golden Pope*. With
this *Golden Mallet* he ftrikes at the *Golden
Door*, which while He was in Doing, there
were Workmen Ordered without to Break
it open, which done, all the *Chips*, *Stones*,
Duft and *Dirt*, (that fell from this *Golden
Gate*, while it was in opening,) are gathered up, and preferved as the choiceft and
moft Ineftimable Relicks ; and as to the
Golden Mallet which this New Pope held in
his Hand, *He* Nobly gave to Cardinal *Sfor-
za* (according to Cuftom) who was his
great Crony and Correfpondent, ofteneft

in

in his Company, and efpecially in moft
Grace and Favour with him, for Lending
him fuch an effectual Lift into *Peters* Chair.
Now let any Man of a Sober Mind Judg,
what kind of Succeffor this prefent Pope is
to *Poor Peter* in his Chair ; the Apoftle *Peter*
faith of himfelf, [*Silver and Gold have I
none,*] Act. 3. 6. But this Pope (his pretended Succeffor) hath *Silver* for himfelf,
and for his *Olympia* too, yea, and a *Golden
Mallet* to give away, *&c.* *Simon Peter* Re-
jected *Simon Magus,* when he would have
Hired of him the Gift of Miracles, *Afts* 8.
19, 20, 23. whereas this *Pope* will do nothing without Ready Money. St. *Peter* paid
his Tribute to Temporal Princes, even at
his Lord Chrifts Command, both for *himfelf*
and for his *Mafter,* *Matth.* 17. 24. to the
laft ; But this *Pope* (being *Antichrift*)
Scorns any fuch Difgraceful Motion, No,
'tis below his Unholy Highnefs to pay One
Penny ; he Received not *Peters* Patrimony
upon any fuch Ignoble Terms : The *Law of
the Land,* faith, *That a Mans Heir is Obliged to pay the Debts,* and to *perform the Du-
ties of the Inheritance,* otherwife the Heir is
Difinherited, and the Inheritance Divided
among the Creditors : But the Popes Canon-Law faith , *Peters Keys of Authority,*
with all the Profits and Emoluments, belong

to

to the *Pope*, who holds them faft in his
Hand ; but as to his *Key of Doctrine*, wherein *He* Taught Univerfal Subjection to Secular Governours, is a Duty no way Incum-
lent upon *Him*; thefe are great Incum-
l rances to Popes, and would be unfuppor-
table Burdens to our Sacred Inheritance :
Yet in this the Pope likes well enough to
Imitate his Predeceffor *Peter* in, He dearly
loves to Catch with his Angling Rod fuch
Fifhes in his *Sea* or *See*, as have a peice of
Silver in their Mouths, *Matth.* 17. 27. and
it will do no Harm,if now and then a peice of
Gold be found there alfo , for then will he be
furnifh'd with Materials,not only for a Silver
Cupboard of Plate, but likewife for making
his *Golden Doors*, and his *Golden Mallets*.

The *Fifth Ceremony* fhould have been,
When the *Golden Door* was opened , He
fhould have proceeded to the *Porphiry*
Chair, the *Chair of Exploration*, where the
Youngeft *Cardinal-Deacon* fhould have Ex-
amined Things and Things. But this Cu-
ftomary Ceremony is now a Days Anti-
quated as Superfluous and Unnecefliary,
fince commonly thofe Popes that have been
lately Elected, had given fufficient proof
by their Baftards of their *Virility*, and that
they were known beforehand to be of the
Right *Mafculin Gender* , and indeed I think

ᶦt need not be much Doubted, but rather
than fail, rather than this Pope fhould have
this trouble given him, *Don Olympia* her
felf might have come in with her Teftimony, and have aﬂured them *Viva Voce*, they
might undoubtedly fpare the Labor of Exploration, for fhe hath had fome Experi-
mental Knowledg (which is the Beft) of
his Manhood and Gallantry.   And now,
when I think of it,   I cannot but Imagine
this *Groping Chair* a very ill advifed Injun-
ction,   however upon this Account,   That
whereas the *Romaniﬅs* do ufually Stile their
Head, *The Lord God their Pope*, now if as
they fay, *He* be indeed a *God*, they do
but Debafe him (if not *Ungod* him) in
Trying whether be be a *Man :*   Methinks
the Words of *Chriﬅ*,   with but a little Vari-
ation, might ferve the pretended *Vicar of
Chriﬅ* :   as the *Lord* did Evidence the Truth
of his Refurrection, by faying,   [*If I be a
Spirit, I ﬂould not have Fleﬂ and Bones,*] Luke
24. 39. So this Vicar might give a Repulfe to
his *Gropers,*by faying,[*If I be a God, I ﬂould not
have Manly Members.*]There is only this Difference,Chriﬅ was willing to beHandled,but *his
Vicar* is *unwilling,* unlefs by *Olympia*, therefore this Rude Ceremony was Omitted.

   But the *Sixth Ceremony* (and fo many there
mult be to comport ftill with the number

of the name of the Beaft, 666.) is a *Cere-mony* of *Ceremonies*, So it fupplies the late omiffion of the *fifth* by way of Redundancy: for this introduceth all the *Splendour* and *Grandeur* of his prime. *Proceffion*, *Confecra-tion,Ccrcnation,*&c. (1) His firft *Proceffion* after his *Election* was thus pompoufly managed : this *great Man*, or rather, this *great God* was mounted upon Mens fhoulders in the moft fplended Equipage imaginable, *fuch* as *Solo-mon in all his Glory was never Arayed with* (for you muft fuppofe this *Pope* to be the goodly *Lilly*, or rather the glorious and gawdy *Tulip*, that our Lord fpeaks of *Matt. 6. 28, 29.*) However *fuch* as neither *Chrift* himfelf (*who was greater than Solomon,* *Matt. 12. 42.*) nor much lefs his Apoftle *Peter* (whofe Succeffour this Pope pretends to be) ever took upon them the like pro-digal and pompious Grandeur. *This Pope was now Arayed in Scarlet Robes, Furr'd with Ermines quite through, and Adorned with the Richeft Gold and Silver Laces, there was pla-ced upon his Head a moft glittering and glori-ous Tripple Crown of Gold, and a moft Rich Collor of Gold all curioufly Enameld with the choiceft Jewels and chiefeft precious Stones : there were put into his Hands two Golden Keys* (pretended to be the fame, that *Chrift* gave to *Peter*, and that *Peter* at his Death be-
queathed

queathed to the *Popes* fucceffively) *which are*
for opening and *fhutting* the *Gates of Heaven*
(a place where Himfelf. is never like to
come) *for whom he pleafeth* : and *over his*
Head was carried a moft ftately Canopy with
lofty, flying, and moft gawdy Streamers, and
He . *Himfelf* under it moft Trim, with his
Artificial Locks finely curl'd and powder'd
with a Vaft Tower or Fruz upon his Fore-
head (in the very Drefs of the *Myftical*
Whore) and in all this Antick Drefs and Pedantick Pageantry, this Pope was prefented
to the people, who (together with his Page)
made thereupon loud Acclamations : [*Vive*
le Papa, Vive le Papa] all along as He made
his Progrefs to *Peters Chair :* mark here,
while this *Apocalyptick Beaft* was thus mounted upon Mens fhoulders, He was then carried like a *Conquerour,* who had now made
a compleat Conqueft over the whole Conclave of his Fellow-Cardinals, and now had
ftoutly Stormed (in defpight of all fraud
and force, yea, of Fate it felf) the pontifical Chair, and in this pofture He was not
onely like King *Saul, who was higher by the*
Head and fhoulders than all the People, but alfo
as a *mighty Nimrod,* who was to Trample
them all under Foot, His Feet ftanding as
high as their Heads : but the moft fignifi-
cant Ceremony in his paffage from the *Gol-*
den

den Hatch or *Wicket*, to his Chair of State,
was this, a lump of Flax was carried before
Him Burning, whereat thefe words were
proclaimed.

——*Sic Tranfit Glcria Mundi.*

'Tis the Prayer of prudent and pious Proteftants, that an happy Blaft may defcend
from Heaven to blow out for ever all this
Antichriftian Glory. Even fo Amen & Amen..
Thus was he brought to his *Chair of State*,
which was likewife covered with *Scarlet*, all
richly Embroidered, Fringed round about
with a Go'd and Silver Silk Fringe, and
glorioufly bedeckt with *Golden Balls* and
Croffes, and which was placed upon as *Lofty*
and as *Coftly* a Throne as was that of *Sel:-
mons*, 1 Kings 10. 18. Thither was he
brougt upon Mens fhoulders, and when
gently taken down (for fear of hurting the
good old Man) there was He *feated*, there
was He *con'ecrated*, and there was He *crowned*, &c. when all this *folemnity* is accom-
plifhed, then His *Herald* (dreffed up in a
Garb comporting with the Pomp) pro-
claims by found of Trumpet, His great
Lord and Mafter, to be now [*the King of
Kings, and Lord of Lords*] and as if that
were not fufficient, *He* had his *Parafites*
prepared

prepared to cry loud [*God Blefs our Lord God the Pope*] Thus *He*, who trode under foot onely the People. before, muft now trample upon the Necks of Kings and Emperours, Inftance onely in *poor Emperour Frederick*, who was conftrained to lay fprawling under the *proud Popes* Feet, on whofe Neck *He* infolently trampled at *Venice* : 'Tis therefore one part of this Pompious Magnificency, that this *Magnifico* hath two Swords ftanding erect by his Chair of State at his right Hand, to denote, that not onely the *Sword of Excommunication*, but alfo the *Sword* of *Civil Dominion* belongs to him alfo : To fay nothing of the number of Gawdy *Beads*, *Agnus Deis* : and abundant more *Remifh Trumpery* expofed to publick View, for the better fetting off the Solemnity of his Inauguration : I think 'twas about well, that, together with his Title aforementioned, this alfo [*God of Gods*] was not fuperadded, fo exalted Him above the *moft High God*, as well as over all *Lords*, *Kings*, and *Emperours.* The *Roman Canon* and Ceremonial Law *commands* the People to fay at the *Popes Inftalment* [*thou art our God the Pope*] and *Pope Martin* could calmly and complaifantly receive the Complement of the *Sicilian* Emballadour faying [*thou art the Lamb of God, that takeft away*

the fins of the World] fo was this, but to det
clare to all the World, that it is He *who fits
in the Temple of God, exalting Himfelf above
all that is called God*, if not above the true
God Himfelf, the Pope dare difpence' with,
if not difannul or contradict the Law of
God: Sure I am, never did any mortal
Man look more like *proud Lucifer* (who faid
ero ficut Altiffimus, I will be like, If not a-
bove; *the moft High*, Ifa. 14. 14.) than this
prefent proud Pope in his pontificalibus expofed to View with all thofe Additional For-
malities did go, all which, yet one more
muft ftill be added, to wit, the *change of his
Name*, his old Name [*Odefchalco* the *Cardinal* muft be turned into *Innocent* the 11*th*.
How *Nocent* this *Innocent* was, the fequel
will demonftrate. Yet follows he the Pattern of *Bocea di Porco* or Hog-face, who was
the *firft Pope* that changed his Name, thus
when his Succeffours were *Cowards*, they
muft be called *Leo*, if he were a Tyrant, called *Clement*, if a *Ruftick*, *Urbanus* though
never fuch a *Turbanus*, or trouble World :
If an Athieft then *Pious*. So if never fo obnoxious, or *Nocent* then it muft be *Innocent*.
The *Popes* of thefe later Years have been generally fhort lived, to Inftance onely in a
few of the laft Edition, Cardinal *Chigi* was
Elected Pope, in the year 55. *April* the
7*th*,

7*th.*, call'd himself *Alexander* the 7*th,* one troublesome enough to the Church, *&c.* He soon trips off (Whether from the goodness of God or his own good Nature, I shall not say) gave up the Ghost, and Resigned up the Chair to Cardinal *Rospigliosi,* who succeeds him *June* 20*th.* by the Name of *Clement* the 9*th,* in the Year 67. The *loss of Candia* afflicted him much more, than the *burntng of London,* and hastened his Death in the Year 70. The Conclave being shut up above Four Months (a long time to be in the Dark, where they made day of Wax Candle, Having neither Windows nor Holes to let in light) at last had so much light as to Elect *Cardinal Altieri,* which was the floating Pope that Created our *Cardinal Howard* (who is after to be mentioned) and then Dyeth in the Year 76. having born the Name of *Clement the Tenth.* So gives place to our *Cardinal Odeschalco,* &c. what a black Character they all bear in the *History of Cardinals,* I must rather request the Reader to observe it there than to expect it here ; especially of this present Pope *Don Olympias* grand Favourite : but above all, I wonder at that Irish Prophet *Malachi* which Dr. *Heylin* mentioneth in his Cosmog. last Edition p. 106.) who lived in the 11*th,* Century, contemporary with *Bernard,* yet undertook

undertook to give an account of all the
Popes from that time to this day, and this
He doth by *Symbols and Hierogliphicks*, and
omitting all others, as befide our purpofe
that which is moft remarkable, is the character, He fo prophetically Impofeth upon
this prefent Pope Symbolically, and in an
Hieroglyphick way plainly Stiles Him,
Bellua Infatiabilis, an *Infatiable Beaft*, I have
been thinking fince I found it that this *Malachi* the *Irifh Prophet* (not to meddle with his
other predictions, *&c.*) hath Accommodated this character fo congruoufly to this
Odefchalco, as if he had been the *Jewifh
Prophet Malachi*, who infallibly had the *Infallible Spirit*, what kind of Spirit (this Popifh Saint, a Ceftertian Monk, Arch-Bifhop
of *Dublin* in *Ireland*) was endued with, is
not eafie to Determine, yet is there found
fuch an Admirable Harmony *inter fignum
& fignatum*, the *Perfon* and the *things* do
Symbolize to Aftonifhment, as *Meffingham;
Buffer*, &c. do obferve.

Conveniunt Rebus Nomina Sæpe Suis.

That this prefent Pope fhould be pointed
out (as by the Finger) to be an *Infatiable
Beaft*, above Five Hundred Years before
He was Born, muft be acknowledg'd *Mira-*

bile Dictu. If ſeveral of the true Prophets of God did ſo Truly Foretel of *Nebuchadnez-zar,* that *He* would Ariſe, and become Gods *Battle-Axe* toHew down theDegenerate Generation of the *Jews,*bring them *to literal Babylon,* keep them Captive there for *Seventy long Years,* &c.   And if ſeveral of the *True Apoſtles of Chriſt* did ſo Truly Foretel of *Antichriſt,* that he would Ariſe out of the *Earth* and out of the *Sea,* and become the *Devils Patriarch* to tread down the outward Court of formal Profeſſours, carry them Captive to *Myſtical Babylon,* keep them in Captivity for *one thouſand two Hundred and ſixty long Years,* &c. And *both theſe,* Some Hundred of Years before they both came to paſs : Why may we not call this *ſtrange Prophet,* (that thus long before foretold of this Individual preſent Pope, that he would Ariſe, and become an *Inſatiable Beaſt)* The Prophet *Malachi the Second ,* notwithſtanding he was one of the *Monkiſh Order,*I cannot but Judg His Teſtimony is therefore ſo much the ſtronger, for 'tis a received Maxim [*firmum eſt probandi Genus quod etiam ab Adverſario Sumiſur , quum Veritas etiam ab Inimicis Veritatis probari poſſit*] 'tis the ſtrongeſt kind of proof, when the very *Enemies of the Truth* are conſtrained to bear Witneſs to it. Hereupon *Ludovicus Vives de probabilitatis Inſtrumentis*

mentis faith thus [*Amici contra Amicum, &*
Inimici pro Inimico Invincibile Teftimonium
erit] which in *plain Englifh* muft thus be *ex-*
plained. The Teftemony of a Papift againft a
Papift, and of a Papift for a Proteftant is a
Teftimony without exception, and more Infallible than this *Infallible Pope*, againft
whom this Popifh Monk, *Malachi*, beareth
fuch an undeniable Teftimony, though his
Friend as of the fame Religion, yet Ho-
nours He Him with no better a Title, than
that of an *Infatiable Beaft*.

The whole Scope of all the following
Difcourfe is no other than a *Defcant* and
Comment upon that *Black* and *Beaftly Brand*,
wherewith this *Irifh* Prophet (*Monk Mala-*
chi) Stigmatiz'd *him* with, fo many Hundred Years before He was in *Rerum Natu-*
rà, or had any Exiftence: Now that He
hath been fo long in his prefent Being, and
hath been Acting (like the *Devils* Patriarch) his Devilifh part in the Tragedy upon the Theatre of the World, ever fince
September the *Twenty-Firft*, in the Year *Se-*
venty Six, whereon He was *Confecrated and*
Crowned, &c. as above. *Time* is always
the beft *Expofitor* of the moft Abftruce and
Obfcure Prophecies; and what a full and
perfect Expofition *Time* it felf hath already
made (and may hereafter make more)
upon

upon this very Text and Title of this *Irifh*
Prophet Malachi, concerning this Pope, is
my Task I have before me to Demonftrate.

Firft, In *General,* That this prefent Pope
is a *Beaft,* is as plain, as if Writ with a Beam
of the Sun upon a Wall of Marble. Seeing
both the *Prophet Daniel,* and the Apoftle
John, do Unanimoufly call the whole Se-
ries of thofe *Roman* Popes no better than
Beafts, yea, fuch Beafts as are beyond
and above all Names, as in the *Preface.*

'Tis manifeft enough even out of their own
Authors (fuch as Wrote the Lives of the
Popes) How that many, if not moft of them,
were *Men* of *Sin* with an Accent ; yea,
Beafts rather than Men ; yea, even *Mon-*
fters in Iniquity : See Dr. *Heylin's* Cofmog.
pag. 106, 107, 108. of the laft Edition,
where you have a Black-Bed Roll of their
State and Story, to the number of Thirty
one, which is a lucky Number, call'd an
even Hitter, and is faid, a Knave and One
and Twenty, (or in plainer Englifh, a
Knave, that ftands for *ten* [*Knaves*] and
One and Twenty more (of the fame litter,
or letter*)* wins all at the Game of Noddy
this Chriftmafs time, wherein *The Knave*
K. of ♦♦♦ is turned up Trump with a witnefs: See alfo *Nefs's Difcovery of Antichrift,*

pag. 56, 57, 58, 59, 60, 61, 62. where you
have a Compendious Landskip of but a few
of the Popes Lives (all gather'd out of
their own *Roman* Writers) to shew in short,
what *Beasts*, what *Monsters of Men* they
have been : And that this great Truth may
be *Compleatly Confirmed* by the Mouth of
even *Three Witnesses*, See also Dr. *Scalter* in
his Comment upon the *Second of Thessalon.*
pag. 115. where he faith, [If a Man may
be so bold with the *Pope*, as *John Baptist* was
with our Saviour (and why should *Christ*
be more Rudely Handel'd than *Antichrist*)
Asking, [*Art thou He that should come, or do
we look for another ?*] The like Answer may
most properly be Returned, [*Go and Tell
what you heard and seen*, to wit, *God is Con-
temn'd, the Devils are Worship'd, Religion is
Prophan'd, Superstition is Hallow'd, Beastly
Lust is Practic'd, and Parricide is not only Per-
petrated, but Patreniz'd,*] with much more
Horrid Hellishness those [*Parùm probi He-
mines.*] or Wicked Popes have done : Is not
this the *Man of Sin*, the *Apocalyptick Beast*,
the *Matchless Monster*, Prophecy'd of in the
Word, that should come into *the World* and
play *Rex*, and his Pranks in it : Now 'tis
below this present Pope to be better than
his Predecessors, He Scorns to Degenerate
from the Worst of them, chusing rather to
Imitate

Imitate them, than Holy *Peter.* The *Irish Prophet* Stiles him a *Beaft* , and *Time* hath proved him fo. Our next Work is to fhew him the *Infatiable* One , for *Craft* and *Cru-elty.*

The *Epithet Infatiable* hath Variety of Ac-ceptions, according to the Variety both of its *Subject* and *Object.* There be various Paffions of the Mind of Man, that are Headftrong, Extravagant and Infatiable, whereby Man is turned into a Beaft, as Thus;

Firft, The *Paffion* of Luft, when it grows Unruly and Ungovernable, *Tranfporting* the Monk out of his Monaftery into the Nun-nery among the Nuns, or fuppofe the Man a *Cardinal,* or a *Pope,* when he is Exported out of all Bonds and Bounds of Tempe-rance and Continency , his *Unruly Luft* caufeth him Rudely to break His *Vow of Chaftity,* and He hereupon Applys himfelf to his common *Curtezans,* or *Don Olympia's,* then is the *Beaft* truly Stiled *Infatiable.* Or

Secondly, When that Paffion of Bloud-Thirftinefs hath the like prevalency over the Mind of Man, makes him as Savage, and as Bloudy-Minded as a Butcher or Beaft, infomuch, that He Delights to Wallow in the Bloud of others, yea, to be *Drunk with*

the

the Bloud of the Saints (which is the Trick of the *Beaſt,*)' then is the Beaſt Rightly Branded with being *Inſatiable,* and then 'tis High Time for good Proteſtants to put up this good Prayer, *Lord. let this Drunken In-ſatiable Beaſt, Spue and Fall, and never Riſe up any more.* or

ˉLaſt.y, (To Omit other Exorbitant Paſ-ſions and Aſſections of Mankind,) the Third Caſe is, When the Connatural Paſſion of Covetouſneſs hath got ſuch a Predominancy. over the Mans Mind, that it Metamorpho-ſes *him* into a *Muck-worm,* yea, into a Mole, that Subterraneal Blind Creature, which lives altogether within the *Earth* (be-ing Reſtleſs, as out of its Center, while out of it) and hath nothing to do with *Heaven* : Muſt Evermore have his Mouth . and Claws full of Earth, when *the Man* will Extract Gain out of a very Dunghil, a Vaſt Revenue for Indulging Stews, and that as a Neceſſary Convenience, [*Ad purgandos Renes*] eſpecially in the Three Hot Months of the Year, when *the Man* doth practical-ly approve of that Motto, [*Lucri bonus eſt odor ex re quâlibet,*] and that other too, [*Lucrum è Lotio eſt Optabile,*] Theſe were the Old Symbols of ſome Great Men of *Rome,* who thought all Gain Sweet, though Got out of the Piſs-Pot, *&c.* And this

Great

Great Man of Rome is no Changling from them, He is for getting the Devil and all, with his *Gain from all Quarters,* Ifa. 56. 11. and Micah 3. 3. *per Tctum,* Then alfo is the *Beaft Infatiable,* and upon this Third Account it is, that the *Prophet Malachi* the Second, aforefaid, calleth in His Characters, this very *Odefchalcho* (the *prefent Pope)* *Bellua Infatiabilis,* as a late Learned Writer doth well Interpret it : Though this *Beaft of Rcme* hath been *Infatiable* enough as is fuppofed, in the Firft Cafe and Account of *Infatiability,* when he look'd upon *Carnal Ccncupifcence* with *Romifh* Spectacles, and according to the Popifh Doctrine, but a *Peccadillo,* a *Trick of Ycuth,* a *Venial Sin;* He had that Flefh-pleafing Circular faying, [*Confefs after Sin, Sin and Confefs,* in Infinitum,] in great Veneration, as a Sovereign Cure for a Popifh Confcience, and indeed, 'tis a wonder that all the *World* (*which lays in Wickednefs,* 1 John 5. 19.) will not eafily turn *Papifts,* that they may Sin, in Sins of all forts, with Peace, wherein they can Blefs themfelves with Pardons prepared and to be Purchafed: But to let that pafs, feeing the Jefuits Rule, [*Si non caftè, tamen cautè*] Anticipates Intelligence of fuch Deeds of Darknefs, till the Pond come to be Scowred again, wherein were found Thoufands of

Infants Skulls, which, as it promoted the, Deſtruction of *Abbeys* here, ſo in Time eve-ry where, yea, of *Rome* it ſelf, that *Bro-thel-Houſe of Babylon*. My Work at preſent is, to give him his due Character of an *Inſa-tiable Beaſt* in both the other Reſpects, with a little Tranſpoſition of the Third, (as coming next to Hand into the Seconds place) to wit, both as a Greedy and as a Bloudy *Inſatiable* Beaſt.

This *Prophet Malachi* (the *Iriſh Monk*) hath *Divine Warrant* to call this Pope an *Inſatiable Beaſt*, ſeeing the *Prophet Iſaiah* calls ſuch *Prieſts* (*ejuſdem Farinæ* of the ſame Brann with this *High Prieſt)* Greedy Dogs, which can never have enough, Iſa. 56. 10, 11. and though they were *dumb Dogs and could not bark*, yet could they bite well enough, perverting the Houſe of God for Prayer into a Den of Cut-Throat Thieves: How far this *Pope* hath been the *Jewiſh Prophets Greedy Dog*, and the *Iriſh Prophets Inſatiable Beaſt*, falls firſt in Order to De-monſtrate: ſo His moſt *Eminent* and *Gain-ful Cheats, whereby he Gulls the ſilly People*, do here follow.

He is (in the General) the Grand *Impo-ſtor of the World*, ſo the *Pope* was call'd by *Doctor Morton* Biſhop of *Durelm* many Yearsago, whoſe Elaborate Book Diſcourſ-eth

eth the many Legerdemain Tricks where,
wirh He *deceiveth Nations,* and all and only
to pick their Pockets.

May we but be let in a little to behold
the Bowels of this *Grand Cheat,* and View
but a while his *Guts* and *Garbage,* 'twill
soon be Discerned that he is the *Devils Par-
triark,* bearing upon his Banner the *Abomi-
nation of Desolation* : The time would fail to
tell, How many Families this *Abominable
Beast* hath made *Desolate* : what else is the
whole Cento and Fardle of Popery , but a
Concatenation of Wiles to compass a purse?
What is the chief Design of this *Balaam of
Roma,* but a continual conjuration for an
House-full of Gold and Silver? Witness his
lying Legends , His *Mock-Miracles , Praying
for the* Dead, and a Thousand more nimble
Tricks too tedious to enumerate, but above
all , His *Doctrine of Purgatory ,* The Fire
whereof doth more effectually *warm the
Popes Kitchin ,* than Torture any Soul He
Damns into it.   'Tis a *Cheat of Cheats* : Methinks the *Apostle Peter* points at this Pope,
(who pretends to be his Successor) while
he speaks of such , as *through Covetousness
with feigned Words,* do make *Merchandise
of Men,* and when He names *Balaam the
Son of Bosor, who loved the wages of Iniquity*
so far, until the *Dumb Ass* forbad the mad-

nefs

ness of the *profane Prophet*, yet *He* cannot
pass off without paying a Divine Doom,
saying, *whose Judgment now of a long time
lingreth, and yet their Damnation slumbreth
not*, 2 Pet. 2. 3. 15, 16. How can it *slumber*
long, when the cry of his cheating Tricks
(together with *that of Bloud*) is gone up to
Heaven to fetch down Gods Vengeance
upon this *Popes* Head, and upon his whole
Popedom : Let the *Apostle Paul* also Joyn
Issue in this matter with his *beloved Peter*,
(both which are represented *Blushing*, as
before, at such pitiful pretended Succes-
sors) who faith likewise [as *Jannes* and
*Jambres withstood Moses, so do these the Mes-
sias, Men of corrupt Minds, and Reprobate
concerning the Faith : But they shall proceed no
further, for their folly shall be made manifest
to all Men, as theirs also was*, 2 Tim. 3. 8, 9.
Now what were *Jannes* and *Jambres*, but
a couple of *Gipsy* or *Ægyptian Conjurers*,
that cheated the People with their *lying
Miracles*, &c. And such have some of the
Popes of Rome (that *Mystical Ægypt*, Rev. 11.
8.) been, &c. [*Habemus Reos Confitentes*]
Popish Authors do acknowledg it, and did
Moses muzzle the Mouths, and made their
Cheats manifest to all Men? How much
more will the *Messias* (who is greater than
Moses, Heb. 3. 3.) confound in due time
                                    this

this *Grand Impcftcr.* 'Tis impoflible for any
Man of a Sober Mind to think otherwife,
efpecially, If he ca.t but a feeing Eye upon [*Taxa Cemeræ Apoftolicæ*] the Apoitoli-
cal Chamber in the Vatican at *Rome*, where
this *Pope* ha*r*h opend his *Pedlars'rack*, expofed all his Vendible Commodities (for *Ro-
mæ Omnia Venalia*) to the beit Advantage
of commending them to his Chapmans Eye,
no Shop fo well furnifhed, or affords fuch
a Tempting Profpect in any of the Walks
of the Royal Exchange Chambers, and that
which gives the moft Splendid and Decoy-
ing Luftre is, there you have the Pope
himfelf in his Grandeur, Courting in Cuftomers, gcod Man, *He* dare not truft his Vaffals, a pack of Knaves, He hath found them
long, wou'd go Snips with their Mafter, He
ha's now Learnt by His Lofs. *Keep the Shop*
Robin, *and it will keep thee.* There himfelf
ftands crying in the very Language of *Folly*
(not of *Wifdcm*) *who fo is fimple, let him
turn in Hither*, Prov. 9. 16. He Cants in his
Profelytes with Pedlars Pedantick Oratory,
Coying them in with come along my *Cro-
nies*, my Soft Pates (for you muft fuppofe
He is of the fame Sentiments with that
Crafty *Shcp-Keeper*, who once Boafted, He
would not fell all his *Children and Fools*, his
Cuftomers, for fome Hundreds of Pounds
in

in the Year) come along my Corculums,
look about you, Gentlemen, what lack
you? Lo, here's a *Goose-Giblet Pye*, wherein
every Palate may pleafe it felf, what will
ye buy? I am juft now upon my laft Legs,
my long Leafe of 1260 Years is now at its
laft Gafp and Expiration, what, never a
packing-penny among you all for a poor
packing-off Pope: But are you Defirous
to know his *Wares* (all very Vendible to the
Credulous, that never think of the Cheat)
what are his Commodities in particular? I
will tell you, where you have them all
named, and we are not a little obliged to
the *Infallible Holy Ghoft*, that will take all
the pains in giving us a Diftinct Catalogue
of all this *Infallible Ghoftly* Fathers Commodities: He tells you, *Rev.* 18. 12, 13. in
Antichrifts Stately Shop, you may have for
Ready Money [*the Merchandife of Gold and*
Silver, precious Stones and *Pearls, fine Lennen*
and Purple, all *Silk* and *Scarlet, all Thyne or*
Sweet Wood, all manner of Veffels of Ivory,
all manner of Veffels of precious Wood , of
Brafs, of *Iron,* and of *Marble* ; yet more,
yea, and *Cinnamon, Odours,* and *Ointments,*
yea, *Frankincenfe, Wine* and *Oyl,* yea, *fine*
Flower and *Wheat,* yet more, there be *Beafts,*
and *Sheep,* and *Horfes,* (I wonder *Affes* are
left out) and Chariots, and Slaves, (no doubt
on't,

on't, but the greateſt Ware is behind) the *Souls of Men.*

IV. Who will not ſay here [God bleſs us] what a Shop is this? So Capaeious, and ſo Accommodated with all the choiceſt and chiefeſt Commodities, that this lower World can afford: Here's the Riches of both the *Indies* (*Gold, Silver,* and *precious Stones there-of*) Here's the Riches of all Countrys and Kingdoms, betwixt *Eaſt* and *Weſt, North* and *South* : Here's the very Quinteſſence and Compendium of *Europe* , of *Aſia,* of *Africk* , and of *America* : is not this the *Grand Impoſtor,* that even call'd for a pack-ing-penny to a poor Pope, who hath ſo much of Treaſure, enough to ſerve himſelf and enough to ſell to others. But I wonder *He* expoſeth his *Scarlet* to Sale, Having ſo much uſe for it to Array the *Scarlet Whore* : as alſo that the *Beaſt* ſhould be a Seller of *Beaſts,* and above all, I wonder what priçe He ſets upon the *Souls of Men* : ſeeing our Lord Chriſt (who beſt knew the worth of Souls, becauſe He onely went to the price of Souls) *Valued one Soul worth the whole World,* Matth. 16. 26. Surely He muſt be the *Antichriſt,* who *ſelleth Souls* for Trifles : In a Word, ſurely, This Pope is *Jack of all Trades* : Here he is a *Goldſmith,* with his Gold and Silver, and it may be a *Banker,* I wiſh

I wifh him to become a *Bankrupt*. Here he
is a *Jeweller*, with his *Pearls* and *Precious
Stones*. Here he is a *Linnen-Draper*, with
his *Fine Linnen* and *Purple*, (I doubt He
wants the *Scotch-Cloth*.) Here you have
him a *Silk-Man* with his Silks of all forts,
and fear not, but he has *Satten* (or *Satan*) enough. Here he is a *Turner*, that
Sells all forts of *Veffels*, wherewith he *Turns*
the World Upfide Down ; this *He* effects by
Veffels of Wrath, but He Sells for *Slaves* the
Veffels of Mercy. Here you have him one
while a *Brazer* with his *Brafs* ; another
while an *Iron-Monger* with his *Iron* ; yea,
fometimes a *Stone-Cutter*, with his *Marble*,
and why not a *Tinker* too, being a Kin to
him, that inftead of mending fome Holes,
made many more, yet was well paid for
his pains. Here he is a *Druggift*, with his
Cinnamon, *Odours* and *Ointment*, &c. not
one Sophifticated Drug amongft them all.
Here he comes as a *Vintner* with his Bottles
of *Wine* to *comfort the Heart*, and his Cruifes
of *Oil* to Chear and Clear the Countenance;
'tis well if there be not a Tincture of the
Wine of Sodom among Hands. Yea, rather than fail , *He* becomes a *Corn-Chand-
ler*, affording you *Wheat*, either broken into *Flour* (with Bran enough in it) or in
the whole Grain, but a little Mufty by laying

ing in a bad Granary or Garner , the A-
poftolical *Chamber.* Yet lower, nay rather
than fit Idle, he will come as a Ruftick
Drover to Sell *Beafts,* and *Sheep,* and *Horfes,* (well Mouth'd and Man'd all, and made
as Tame as *Affes.*) And at laft he comes as
a *Coach-Maker,* who has his *Charots* to Sell,
but have a care they carry you not to *Purgatory* inftead of *Abrahams Bofom.* But to
Crown up the Catalogue of all his Commodities, Note, that which we Read *Slaves,*
doth fignifit [*Bodies,*] which he Sels for
Slaves, and the *Souls of Men* too. And fo
Laftly, he becomes a *Body-feller,* and (to
make a thorough-whole-fale Trade, a *Soul-
feller* alfo. Let us all (with *Mofes*) turn
afide to fee this *great Wonder,* fure I am, never did *Proteus* turn himfelf into fo many
Shapes, never did any *Jefuit* (this *Popes*
Creature) Convert himfelf into fo many
Callings, as His Mafter is here Reprefented in. The Pope hath made a Monopoly
of all Employs to himfelf, both in *City* and
Country. And the greateft Merchants Shop
(whofe Riches lay not there, but in the
Warehoufe) cannot, though taken both
together, be compared to the *Apoftolical
Chamber.* One coming into a Merchants
Shop (I knew the Man, a Ruftick Carri-
er) and feeing no Goods therein, Bluntly
Asks

Asks the Apprentice (fitting alone in the
Shop) what was Sold there? the Malapert
Youth Anfwered, We Sell *Loggerheads,* fay
you fo, faith the Ruftick, Then you have
a Quick Market for them, feeing I fee but
One left in the Shop.   There is no Danger
of any *Citizen* or *Countryman* either *Miffing*
(what Wares he would be at) or *Miftakings*
of that Nature, for here's all things Expofed
to View.   There is yet One Mifchief mention'd, *Revel.* 18.11. where (this Rich Shop
is Inventory'd) that *No Man Buyeth His*
Merchandife any more : . This will break him
at laft.

   But let my Countrymen take thefe Two
Cautions,

  Firft, Have a care of a Cheat in his corrupt Commodities : for he fells them all in
a very dark Shop, not fuffering you to ex-
ercife your own Reafon ; you muft take
all upon his crack'd Credit, and comply
with His price in an *Implicit Faith,* and in a
blind Obedience you muft believe what the
Pope believes, and he is no fuch Fool as to
difcommend his own Wares, He beft Em-
braces Blindfold Buyers, *Ignorance is the Mo-*
ther of his Merchandize.

  The Second Caution is, 'Tis dangerous
venturing into this *Apoftolical Chamber,* leaft
this *Grand Cheat* pick your pockets, for
                though

though his Wares be naught, being all
for Impofitions, *He* will impofe them upon
you, and he will not truft you to the door
for fear you give him the flip, He muft
have *Ready Money* paid down upon the nail.

Have a care you be not cox'd out of good
Gold for bad Ware : And before you *Saddle*
your *Afs* to Ride down to this Arch Huxter in Myftical *Ægypt*, let me befeech you
to confider a little in your confidering Cap,
whither it were not far better for you, to
make your Buying Bargains with *Chrift*
than with *Antichrift* , for the *former* Invites
Chapmen to buy his *true Treafure, unfearch-
able 'Riches, Gold Tryed in the* Fire, *Royal
Robes* of his own Righteoufnefs, the choiceft
Opthalmicks or *Eye-Salve*, the *Waters of
Life,* the *Wine of the* Spirit, the *Milk* of
Coufolation, &c. And all thefe *without Money*
and without *Price,* Ifa. 55. 1. Rev. 3. 18.
Eph. 3. 8. Ifa. 66. 11, *&c.* but the *latter*
Wheadles *fimple ones* (as above) to buy his
Trafh and *Trumpery*, yet credulous Fools
muft part with much Money , and a prodi-
gious price for them, *&c.*

But fome may fay, thefe *Commodities* of
the *Pope,* as fet down in the *Catalogue* under
fuch Glittering Titles , *Rev.* 18. 12, 13.
Gold, Silver, &c. look nothing like to *Trafh*
and *Trumpery* : To this I anfwer, the Book
of

of the *Revelation* is fo Abftrufe and My
rious, that it requires another *Revelatic*
unfold its Myftery : I confefs, I have c
fulted fome Learned Interpreters upon
place: But that which is *Inftar Omni*
and gives a None-Such Interpretation is
chief Auditor of the Apoftolick Chambe
his Infallible Account Book.

Never did the *profoundeft Interpreter* (
not the Accuteft of their own *Popifh Poftil*
make a plainer Explanation of any C
Scripture, than this Popes *Auditor* G
ral hath made of *Rev.* 18. 12. 13. All
Voluminous Quirks of the moft Mercu
Jefuits [*Cajetan, Mendoza, Salmeron,* &
are comparatively but Infiped Stuff,
dull Defcants to that one *Auditors Recor*
the Romifh Merchandife in this Popes A
ftolical Chamber. Yea, the *Chaldee Paraphi*
or *Onkelos* (fo much cry'd up in the Wo:
is but a *Jejune Piece* to it. *This* is the *M*
Piece of all, wherein what be the *Re*
Fearls and precious Stones, &c. are mad
Legible and *Intelligible*, that every comr
Capacity may both *Apprehend* and *Com*
hend the right Notion of them.

In that known Court-Rolls and ⟨R
Book, is Regiftred, and made publick
common and current Price of a many-ch
and curious Commodities; as *Pardons*,
                                        dig

dulgences, *Licenses*, *Absolutions*, &c. whatever you have a mind to buy : Indeed the
Crys of Vendible Wares in the Streets of
London [*will you buy this*, &c. *and will you
buy that*, &c.] are both [πλυωση and
ᴅ ᴠᴏᴍᴊᴀ] *manifold* and somewhat hard
to be underſtood, eſpecially in ſome of the
cryes : but the *cryes* and *outcryes* in the *Streets
of Rome*, do far exceed the beſt of *curs*, yea
that of *Dainty Trotters, Curious Trotters:* But
they that have a mind to *Trot* to *Rome*, may
There hear far better *Crys*, as this for one
[*will ye buy any Bodies*, *will ye buy any
Souls of Men?*] This is a Raree-Show Indeed, and ſuch a *Tickling*, *Tempting Cry*,
as will cauſe empty Houſes, who would not
Run out (though the Pot be boiling upon
the Fire, and the Spit turning at it) to ſee
the *Wonders of the Beaſt ?* Revel. 13. 3, 13,
14. Who would not but deſire to be a
Chapman for (at leaſt to Cheap) his Rare
Commodities?

But becauſe it may ſeem a little below
His *Highneſs* and *Holineſs*, to become a common Cryer, He hath learnt the Trick of
our Nimble *Quacks* and *Don Quick-Sots* ;
as every common *Quack* and *Mountebank*,
Prints now his Bills, Hands them out *Gratis*
with much Generoſity, yet catches *Children
and Fools* enough to pay for them ; there

you have set down, *Elixir Vitæ* at so much,
Elixir Salutis at so much ; the *Golden Spirit*
at so much, the *Scurvy Spirit* at so much,
Sovereign Powder for so much, the *Plaister*,
call'd *All-Heal*, for so much, and Twenty
Rarities more (all *Arcanums*) none At-
tains to such a Secret as himself ; every
thing Exposed is good for all things, if but
a *Thumb-Bottle* of his Liquor be Bought,
'twill Cure all Diseases; if but a little of
his Balsom be Applied , 'twill Heal all
Wounds. What *Madmen* be these to be either Slain or Lie in the midst of so many
Antidotes, *&c.* Yea, the *Mountebank* goes
a little further, He comes forth *Cum Regis*
Privilegio, makes Experiments upon himself, both in *Stabbings* and *Poisonings*, Builds
his Theatre , whereon he Exposeth all his
Cheating Tricks to Publick View, and when
the Credulous come not in fast enough to
make their Markets there, his *Merry-An-*
drew must Dance upon a Rope, play Twenty pretty Pranks (yet all the while more
Knave than Fool) to Decoy them, and
yet when all is done, few more than the
Rabble are Caught in the Snare.
   So this *Grand Quack* the *Pope*, and *Ma-*
ster-Mountebank, Prints his Bills *Cum Privi-*
legio, commends to the Life his Cursed
Wares, Acts all the parts of the former to
a Threed

a Threed, yet Advances upon an Higher Stage. And indeed, His Wares have a ftrange Operation. If but a *Thumb-Bottle* of his *Wine of Fornication* be Drunk, it will ftrangely Intoxicate even the *Kings of the Earth.* And his *Jefuits Powder* will work Wonders.

But not to detain you in the Dark any longer, If you have a mind to be Cheated, or only to fee his Cheats, you'l find *his Printed Bills,* Publifh'd to the whole World with *Antichrifts Arms* ftamp'd upon them, in his *Taxa Cameræ Apoftolicæ,* where you have the *Scarlet Whore's Adulterated* Wares particularly Reprefented, both in their *Species, Properties, Profits* and *Prices,* yea, and there is *Morfus Diaboli,* the Herb call'd *Devil-bit,* to wrap them up in, caft into the Bargain.

Take only an *Antipharmacon,* a *Divine Allay* and *Prefervative,* along with you, leaft your Noftrils be offended, and your Vital and Animal Spirits contract any Tincture of Contagion, while I am (to fatisfic your Curiofity) but a little way *Digging* into this *ftinking Dunghil.* I have good Warrant for this my good Work, in laying open the Cheating Abominations of this *Scarlet Coloured Beaft.* As that *Man of God,* great *Elijah* could not tell how to *Ridicule* enough

the Prophane *Priefts of Baal*, 1 Kings 18.
27. Much more may I *Ridicule* the Grand
Mafter of them, and this cannot be better
done, than by giving you but a brief Landskip of the *Roman* Merchandize, a bare
Recitatim whereof is a fufficient *Refutation*
to any Sober and Right Thinking Mind.

The *Apoftolical Chamber* Pofts up its [*Si*
Quis, &c.] *If any one* want this or that
Popifh Trumpery, they may *come* and be
welcome at this *prefent Popes* Ware-houfe, pro-
vided always they come with Money in
their Hands, and come up to the current
Price (by Canon-Law) of each Vendible
Commodity : come along my Hearts, *My*
Son, Give me thy Heart. You fhall have
Robin Hood Penniworths, enough for your
Money in all Confcience : becaufe you are
all Friends, you fhall all be very Kindly
Ufed, and fo *Farewel.*

A Schedule or Lift of the *Romifh* Wares,
this *Pope* (the *Lord* of the *Manour*) Expofeth to Sale by Inch of Candle, take as
followeth,

Imprimis, He Expofeth his Pick-pockering
Pardons of all forts and fizes, and the Prices
thereof (in fome of them) are fet down
in Black and White upon the Popes Tables
hung out to Publick View, or fomething
Equivalent. As

Firft,

Firſt, A *Pardon* for the Third part of your Sins, equally Divided by Indifferent Perſons, for Seven Pound Ten Shillings, and if you would Buy off the other Two parts, 'twill Coſt you Two and Twenty Pound Ten Shillings, and a very Rich Penniworth.

Secondly, A *Pardon* for Forty Eight Years Sins, as you can Agree with this *Innocent Pope*; He is a very *Innocent*, you may poſſibly Wheadle him to your own Terms with Nuts and Apples, *&c.*

Thirdly, A *Pardon* for Two Thouſand Eight Hundred Years, confirm'd by Pope *Paſchal* the Firſt, by *Boniface* the Eighth, and by *Gregory* the Ninth, and now under a New Ratification by this Pope *Innocent* the Eleventh ; this may be had Dog-cheap, only for ſaying a few very ſhort Prayers in the right Critical Hour, betwixt the *Elevation* of the Hoſt and Three *Agnus Dei's* ; This would keep you out of *Purgatory* for a long time upon eaſie Terms.

Fourthly, A *Pardon* for Thirty Three Thouſand Years at a very low Rate, only for once going up a pair of Stairs, which, you muſt ſuppoſe, were the very ſame that Chriſt Aſcended, when he appeard before *Pontius Pilate.* Here's *great Wages* for a *little Work* ; and he's a Fool in Grain, that will not Purchaſe ſuch a cheap Pardon for fo long a Time, provided he may have *general Warranty* for fecuring his Bargain till that Time be Expir'd; and much more of this Trafh, *&c.*

* *Item, Abfolutions* of various Prices, according the Crime committed. As

Firft, For *Sacriledg.*, Ten Shillings and Six Pence.

Secondly, For *Symony* in a *Prieft* the fame Price, but in a *Lay-Man* the odd Eighteen Pence fhall be Baited. Kindly done.

Thirdly, For *Perjury*, 'tis a Rich Pennyworth at Nine Shillings.

Fourthly, For *Murder*, If it be a Prieft that is Kill'd, it cannot be Dear at one [Two Pence] more than a *Mark*, I would never be a Prieft there, where my Life is no higher Valued. But you may Kill your *Father, Mother, Wife* or *Sifter*, &c. upon eafier Terms, That fhall but coft you Ten Shillings and Six Pence.

Fifthly, For *Adultery*, Deflouring a Virgin goes at Nine Shillings, but *Inceft* with Mother, Sifter, *&c*, is cheaper, paffing at Seven Shillings and Six Pence. And the *Whore* that Deftroys her Baftard Child either before or after Birth, hath the felf fame Sum to pay.

Sixthly, For *Burning a Neighbours Houfe* is Dog-cheap at Twelve Shillings; but for

Burning

Burning Heretical Cities, 'tis severely Pu-
nish'd with being *Canoniz'd for Saints*,
&c.

Item, Licenses for what you List.

First, If you be a Priest you may keep
a Whore, paying only Ten Shillings and
Six Pence; and if a Lay-Man it will cost
you no more; that the one may not De-
ride the other.

Secondly, A *Licenfe* to be Lazy, and to
become an *Abby-Lubber*, and so to be *Inutile
pondus Terræ*, Living there like Hogs in the
Stie, unuseful to Mankind, unless to the
Wanton Nuns.

Thirdly, A *Licenfe* to be Licentious, and
to have the liberty of the Stews the Three
Hot Months of the Year, there is the *Roman Recipe* prescrib'd (with Dr. Pope's
probatum est) *ad purgandos Renes*. This
Grand Quack, or great *Mountebank*, is
Tender of his *Profelytes* Health, Allows this
Remedy (which God never thought of,
when he said, *'Tis not good for Man to be
alone*, Gen. 3. 18.) to prevent his Popelings (under the *Vow of Chaftity*) from
falling into Acute Fevers, and to shew how
good Natured he will be to them (Re-
membering it had been his own needful Priviledg and Practice) you may have these
Two last Licenses (both to be *Lazy* and to
H 4   be

be *Licentious*) *Gratis*. Gra-Mercy upon his Kind Heart, they shall not cost you
a Penny.

Fourthly, Yet a *Licenfe* to *Eat Flesh-in
Lent*, will cost you much more, for his Un-
Holinefs Infallibly Judgeth this to be a far
greater Sin *than to keep a Whore*. Yea, and
many more *Indulgences*.

Item, Here you may have *Holy Water*
Chymically prepared, *Secundum Artem Di-
abolicam*, for driving away the Devil; hence
comes that Popish Proverb, to exprefs
fomething that is *Hateful*, [*A Man loves it
as well as the Devil loves Holy Water.*] You
muft fuppofe, *that Water* which the Pope
Conjures into the like *Holinefs* with his own,
is able to Conjure away the ftrongeft Devil
in Hell.

Item, You may have *Holy Oil*, compounded according to the fame Art, only
'tis an *Arcanum* and *Magifterial*. The Pope
hath been fo kind to let the World know
how he makes his *Holy Water*, Piffing it out
by Conjuration; but *he* hath a mind to be
private in Confecrating his *Holy Oil*, and
when he hath done his beft to it, have a
care you eat it not with a *Romish* Sallet,
leaft it be mix'd with *Jefuits Powder*; however, 'tis good enough to Liquor your
Boots after your long Journey to *Rome*.

No

No doubt but it serves notably as an Unguent for (far better than for *anointing the Sick* to make them well) the *Popes Charet Wheels*, makes them run glib in all Transmarine Countreys, and is now calling for a waft over into ours ; do not you hear Him at *Callice*, Crying, *have over for* Dover, *have over for* England : God grant Him contrary Winds , but if the *Prince of the Air* must be permitted to lend Him a lift with a *Favonian* or Favourable Wind, God grant, this proud Mystical *Pharaoh* of *Spiritual Ægypt*, Rev. 11. 8. May meet with no better a *Fate* and *Fare*, than that *Litteral King of Ægypt did*; who, though for ought we know to the contrary, had as fair *way* and *weather* into the midst of the *Red Sea*, as *Israel* had, yet when Irrecoverably brought into an unavoidable Noose (which He could not Slip nor Retreat from) then *God looked out of the black* side of the Cloud (which was *towards His Host*, as the *bright side was toward* Israel) with an angry Countenance, took off His *Charet Wheels*, made them (though never so well Oyled with *His Priests Holy Oyl) drive Heavily*, then dows'd Him with a Witness, and drown'd Him (too) with a Vengeance, *Exod.* 14. 7. 20. 22, 23, 24, 25, *&c.* I cannot but be confident, that the Lord will look through this

black

black cloudy Dispensation, with a *look of Love* upon his own People (as he did upon *poor, perplexed Peter*, Luke 22. 61.) and with a *look of Wrath* upon this great *Leviathan*, His *Holy Oyl* shall fail. His *Chariot Wheels*, and they shall never become as the *Chariots* of *Aminadab*, *England* cannot ever be a *willing People* to Receive Him :

Item, Here you may have His *Holy Salt* also, this is soundly *Conjur'd* likewise into as good an Holiness as that of His *Holy Water*, or as that of His *own Holiness* : and with this *Holy Stuff* the *Beast* works His Mighty Miracles and Wonders : What place soever hath this *Holy Salt* scattered upon it, neither the *Devil* nor any of his *evil Spirits* have any power against it : 'Tis a wonder there should be so many Houses, Haunted with Hobgoblins all over His *Holinesses Dominions* , Surely, either His *Holy Salt* hath lost its efficatious Vertue, or *Himself* hath lost the Right Art to Consecrate it, or more likely, the Devil is in His Priests that they improve it not. 'Tis a wonder this *old Sophister* doth not dash whole handfuls of this *Holy Salt* in the Eyes of those Raw *Freshmen* (those *Novices* as he calls the *Protestants*) and so to blind them for ever. But though this will not do *(His Holy Salt* having lost its Efficacy) He hath a better Trick behind

far

far more Bloudy, He would *Bleed* and *Burn*
thofe He cannot *Blind*: If His *Holy Salt have*
loft its Savour (as indeed it hath,) otherwife
there could never have been fo much Car-
rion, for want of Seafoning, both among
Popes and His Popelings) what is it good to,
but to be *caft to the Dunghil*, and to be
Troden Underfoot? Matth. 5. 13. *England* is
as the *Garden of 'Eden*, never any *Pope* that
pafled through the *Porphury Chair* (ever
fince the *Writ of Ejectment* was by an Almighty Hand Served upon Him to difpoflefs
that Devil in the Reformation) but He hath
lick'd his Lips, and longed after fome fweet
Lettuces, that Grow in this *Englifh Garden,*
God grant it may be, as the Law calls that
Writ, an *Ejectione Firmæ* : that this *evil Spi-*
rit (once caft out) may not find the *Houfe*
of our Land (which, God knows is now
neither *Swept* of Moral Vices, nor *Garnifh:d*
with Moral Vertues, but too much over-
fpread with Epidemical Immortality) *empty*
alfo of all Grace, and fo Return with *Seven*
worfe Spirits than the former, Matth. 12. 43,
44, 45. I would to God, *England* were not
fo much like *Jericho* , *whofe Situation was*
pleafant, but the Waters were naughty : Our
frefh River of *Thames* feems to Run fo near
the falt Waters of *Tybur* (ever fince the
Beaft fouled our Fountains with his Feet,
                                             Ezek.

Ezek. 34, 18.) that they ta.. a little *Brackiſh*
and ſomewhat Imbib'd with the *Salt-Sea of*
Rome, 'Iis too much Tinged with the
Tincture of its *Holy Salt*, Oh where is that
Eliſha, that will take a Cruſe of *better Salt*
(than this *Popes Holy Salt* is) happily to
hand in, that our *Waters may be Healed*, &c.
2 Kings 2 19, 20, 21.

   Item, Here is expoſed to Sale the *Holy Milk*
of the *Virgin Mary*, which, ſome of the Popes
Doctours affirm, is as Sovereign and Salvi-
fical as the Bloud of her Son our Saviour.
However, 'Tis commended moſt Highly for
never-failing to cure Conſumptions, far exceeding the Milk of an *Aſſe*, or that of the
Red-Cow. What Fools are the Conſumptive and Phtiſical Popelings, that have ſuch
a Ready Cure by them, yet ſo many dye
of a *Conſumption*, which is ſo *Ranting* and
Regnant a Diſeaſe in thoſe *Hot Climates*:
Nay, What a Fool is the Conſumptive *Pope*
or *Antichriſt* himſelf, who doth not by this
truſty trick diſapoint the Divine Doom paſ-
ſed upon him, what need he Fear [*that the*
Lord ſhall CONSUME Him with the Spirit of
his Mouth.] 2 Theſſ. 2. 8. Seeing an Hearty
Draught of this *Holy Milk* will cure the Conſumption : This Pope might then ſay as one
of his Holy Predeceſſours once ſaid, I will
have my Will [*Al deſpito di dio*] in De-
                  ſpight

spight of God ; But the mischeif is, neither
the Pope nor his Popelings dare take a sufficient Dose of this Salutiferous Antidote, for
fear of marring the General Market hereof,
'tis a long time since the Blessed Virgin gave
her Milk, and they can expect none in her
Glorified Breasts, the *old Stock* (suppose every one take but a little sup, though that is
not enough) must needs be far spent in
above Sixteen Hundred Years, and where
or how these Traders make their *old Store*
bring in *new*, I know not, unless that *Image*
of the Virgin (which bid *Bernard Good Mor-*
row at his entrance into the Church, and
whom that Father Rebuked, because She a
Woman, took upon her (contrary to the
Truly Apostolical Canon) to speak in the
Church, might supply , for that Idol of
Stone might equally and as Probably have
Milk in its Breast as well as a *Voice in its*
Mouth : But that which spoil'd the expecta-
tion of this fresh supply of *Holy Milk*, was
the Discovery of a crafty Priest that was
crept into the Hollow Belly of this Holy
Image, and that gave Holy *Bernard* the
Hearty Salutation , and sure I am, there
could not be much *Holy Milk* in such a Pro-
fligate Priests Breast, who durst put such an
affronting Cheat upon so Holy a Father.
But suppose there were supply then, 'tis
                                                    above

above 500 Years ago, and this cry [*will ye
have any holy Milk,* &c.] that Milk-street
Market muſt needs be down ere now, ſeeing all their *Milk-Maids* (whereof they
cannot have many, while the Indulged Stews
afford his Unholineſs ſuch a vaſt Revenue)
are now ſurely ſitting upon their Empty
Pales: But I had forgot my ſelf that the
Beaſt can work Wonders, and can multi-
ply that *Holy Milk* (though but little from
the Bleſſed Virgin) as well as Chriſt did the
Barly Loaves; Yea, He hath done it to ſuch
an overflow, that the Prieſts (all the Popedom over) do expoſe this *Holy Milk* to Sale,
all pretending that theirs is the very Milk
of the *Virgin Mary*, which, were all they
have in their Conſecrated Dairys gathered
together into one place, *Solomons* prodigious
Molten Sea could not poſſibly contain it.
Nay, hereby they put the greateſt Diſho-
nour upon the Holy Mother of our Lord
(whom they pretend to Adore) in making
Her ſuch a *Milk-Beaſt*, as *Ten* of the beſt
Cows in *Holland* cannot give the like quan-
tity in Ten Years,

    Item, Holy-Bread is here to be had: The
Pope (good Man) takes care for your
Table, and to furniſh it ſo far as *Holy Water,
Holy Oyl, Holy Salt, Holy Milk,* and *Holy
Bread* will go : But ſurely all theſe do but
                                          look

look like a Lent Dinner, I hope his Holiness
keeps a better Table for Himself: If you
be a *Water Drinker*, here's the belt of the
Kind, *Holy Water* for you, of the Popes
own *making*, I should have said, *Consecrating*:
If you be a *Milk-Sop*, Here's the belt of
the Kind, Holy *Milk*, the self same your
Saviour Sucked out of the self-same Breasts,
when he was a Child, and who will not be
content with the same Fare that Bred the
Blessed Babe of *Bethlehem*, the *Holy Child
Jesus*, and because the *Master* of this *Lent-
Feast*, will not undervalue you as a sort of
sorry Sucklings, He is so *Kind-hearted* as to
allow you *Bread* to your *Milk*, that you
may *sup* it and not *suck* it, is not *b..ing* and
supping good Fare? especially, of *Holy
Bread* and *Holy Milk.* You must not expect
a Glass of Wine, for I find not any *Holy
Wine* in the *Popes Ware-shop.* Perhaps he and
his *Priests* Monopolizes it wholly to themselves, for in the Eucharist, the Cup is forbid to you of the Laity, you must suck
Wine out of the *Bread*, If you would have
it, and can catch it.

Neither must you grudge that you have
onely Bread (though it be but course Bar-
ley Bread, such as you were never possibly
brought up with) 'tis however *Holy Bread*,
and the *Holier*, and so more satisfactory,
because

becaufe (as this *Mart-Mafter* tells you)
'tis a *Fragment* of thofe fame *Five Loaves*
wherewith *Chrift* fed the *Multitude*,
and picked out of the Twelve Baskets
(*that were taken away*) by fome of the
Popes nimbleft Snips, but I wonder how
they have kept it from Moulding ever fince,
The *Moulded Bread* wherewith the *Gibeonites*
cheated *Jofhua*, was not fo many *Hours* old,
as this *Holy Bread* is *Years*, at this Day. If
it be *Sound Bread* that is fhewn you, take
heed you be not cheated with it, as *Jofhua*
was with the *Mauldy* : But you will fay,
why is *Holy Salt* prepared for the Table,
when the forementioned Fare needs it not ?
Anfwer, You muft know 'tis not fet there
for Fafhion-fake onely, as ordinarily, for

   Item, Here you may have *Holy Fifh* too,
and of the felf-fame *two Fifhes* wherewith
Chrift Fed the Multitude alfo, the *Bread*
and the *Fifh* were taken out of the fame
Baskets ; and if you fuppofe it *Frefh Fifh*,
then there is ufe for your Salt, but to prevent your *Second* Objection about the ufe
of your *Oyl*, you muft rather fuppofe it
Holy Fifh Salted with that *Holy Salt*, (it
could never have otherwife kept fo long,
fweet for this Sixteen Centuries) and then
your *Holy Oyl* will make your *Holy Fifh* (fo
called) flip down the better, and be mo-
                    difh

difh enough, and what would you have more, is not here enough for a *Four Penny Ordinary.*

Item, Befides this Belly-Timber, here you are Treated with a Numberlefs Number of *Rarieties.* As

Firft, The *Affes* Tail upon which Chrift Rode; not a word of his *Ears.*

Secondly, *Jofephs Breeches* both Thread-bare and out of Fafhion, they will do you neither Credit nor Service.

Thirdly, A Feather from the Cock that Crew, and awaken'd *Peters* Confcience; yet this Startles not *Peters* Succeffor for his Apoftacy; as alfo a Feather from *Grabriels* Wing, taken up at fuch a time when as Angels caft their Feathers.

Fourthly, Choice Hair Cloth, the fame as *Elijah* and *John Baptift* wore, good enough for the Pope to do Penance in, for forcing the Witneffes into Sack-Cloth.

Sixthly, Whole Cart Loads of *Apoftles Bones,* fometimes thofe of a Thief (as once) drops in among them; good for I know not what.

Item, Sold at a very Reafonable Rate,

Firft, An Holy Rag clip'd off from Chrifts Seamlefs Coat; 'tis a wonder how the Pope got it from the Soldier to whom it fell by cafting Lots, and 'tis a wonder they

I   have

have not clip'd it all awa
time.

Secondly, The Holy Relick (
Slippers Chrilt wore, when He,
ry with *walking about doing Go*
his Shoes, for the eafe of his F
they were made of well Tar
that lafts ftill; and are not Ro
ere this Day, and I wonder th
expofe them, and not Monopo
himfeif, for they cannot want
Cure his Goury Golls: 'Tis
hear nothing of his Shooes (in
Warehoufe) the Latchets whe
Baptift (though the *Greateft*
men.) thought himfelf Unwor
loofe, *Matth* 11. 11. *Luke* 3. 1

Thirdly, The very *Linnen*
which *Chrift* was wrap'd in the
as likewife that wherewith Chr
Difciples Feet. I am thinking t
Cries in our Streets, [*Here's you*
ing Linnen Cloth,] might do g
in this *Romifh* Market.

Fourthly, The very *Needle*
Work-Basket and *Sciffers*, of the I
which would be excellently u
Exchange-fhop, and could not
in a whole fhoal of Chapmen,
the Pope comes by all thefe Ri

dities for all kind of Cuftomers, is the Que-
ftion? But the Infallible Tradition of the
Church mult be the Satisfactory and Si-
lencing Anfwer.

Item, Laftly, Here you may have, whatever your Heart wifhes, or Need doth Require. Is it any of thofe many things mentioned in *Revel*. 18. 12, 13. Rich all, here
they are to be had. Want you *Holy Bells*
(Baptized with God-Fathers and God-Mo-
thers) God Blefs our Empty New Erected
Steeples, *&c*. Or want you *Holy Beads*,
made of *Glafs, Wood, Stone, Coral* or *Am-
ber* ; *Holy Wax* for your Candles ; *Holy
Knives* for Cutting Hereticks Throats ; or
Holy Rofes, this *Chriftmas* time, a Rare *Prefent* for *Princes* ; or what elfe foever, all is
Holy that comes from his Unholinefs ; and
all have a Power to drive away the Devil,
yet the Devil takes moft of thofe that are
taken with thefe [*Piæ Fraudes*] *Holy
Cheats*. None of their *Names are Writ in
the Lambs Book*, Revel. 13. 8. God Blefs
every good *Englifhman* from the *Beaft* and
his Cheating Tricks.

Having taken a fhort profpect of the
Craft of this *Infatiable Beaft* (to keep clofe
ftill unto the *Irifh Malachi's* Character of
this *prefent Pope*) let us now take a brief
View of his *Cruelty*. He is a molt Accom-

plifh'd *Beaſt,* his *Infallible Unholineſs* is De-
ſcribed by an Infallible Hand (the Spirit of
Truth himſelf) in his moſt Horrible Accou-
trements, no leſs than *Seven Heads to Plot
with,* for the more *crafty* carrying on of
all his *Gainful Cheats,* and no leſs than *Ten
Horns* to *puſh his Plots endway with,* and to
puſh all down (that ſtand in his way)
with *Unparrallel'd Cruelty.* To pretermit all
former Bloudy Plots in foregoing Ages of
this preſent Popes Predeceſſors, againſt all
Proteſtant Countries, ever ſince the Reformation, and againſt *England* in particular,
both in *Queen Elizabeth's, King James's,* and
in *King Charles's* the Firſt's Time. I ſhall
confine my ſelf to Characterize this *Inſatiable Beaſt,* the *Devils Patriarch,* that now
Poſſeſſeth the *Roman Omnipotency.*

His Name is *Innocent* the *Eleventh,* who
after his Inſtalment, was Arrayed with a
White *Surplice,* wherein he Worſhip'd that
God which had now Conſtituted him the
Univerſal Monarch ; in this White Garment he ſeem'd as pure as *Innocence* it ſelf,
there was nothing ſurely under it , but
Meekneſs, Gentleneſs, and Lamb-like *Innocency.* You might then ſtroke the *Beaſt, He*
would not ſpurn you, you might put your
Hand into his very Mouth, *He* by no means
would Bite you. No, *He* had newly put
on

on the Name of *Innocent.*, and He was
(.what ever he had been while a *Cardinal*)
now become an *Innocent Pope*, a Toothlefs
Innocent Milk-Sop, that would neither Kick,
nor Fling, nor Scratch, nor Bite ; but the
mifchief was, *He* foon after going to his
Court-Office, *De propagandà Fide* to a *Confult* there, coming thither without his White
Garment (that Reach'd down to his Foot)
His *Red Shoes,* and *Red Stockins,* were there
Unhappily Difcovered. At that *Confult He.*
Declar'd his Determinations, That he Re-
folv'd (*Adjuvante Diabolo*) to Reduce all
the Heretical Countreys in *Europe* into the
Subjection of His *Roman See,* and He faid
(for a flying Argument) 'twas below *both*
his *Highnefs* and his *Holmefs* to prove fuch a
poor Puny, as his Predeceffors, in playing
fuch fmall Games as they had done ; He
would (for his part) *Take New Meafures,*
and *Make fuch Methods,* as neither God nor
Devil could be able to Difapoint him of his
Defign. Whereupon for the better *Propoga-
tion of his Popifh Faith,* He *propofeth* thefe
following Expedients, and not only fo, but
Impofeth them alfo upon that his *Privy-Coun-
cil,*.who dare not gain-fay their God.
.. The *Firft Propofal Impofed,* was this, *Go
forth* you my *Emiffaries,* and Debauch the
Heretical Countreys, Foift your *Loofe Prin-*

I 3 *ciples,*

ciples, (Calculated for, and Accomodated
to, the Depraved Natures of Mankind in
general) this will foon bring Men to *Loofe
Practices*; 'Tis found by Experience (faith
He in great Gravity, comporting with his
Grandeur) a *Profperous Bait* to Catch, and
a *Powerful Hook* to Hold whole Shoals of
Profelites. I am a *Fifher of Men*, as my
Predeceffor *Peter* was, yet I have a Trick,
which He (fimple Fifher-man) never
thought of, or Practic'd; I can make Men
Atheifts in their Lives, and then they will
turn *Papifts* the fooner, for ftopping the
Mouths of their Natural Confciences
(which will be Barking) the better with
my precious Pardons; whereby I can make
the worft of Sins Venial, *&c.*

The *Second Expedient* propounded by this
Pope there was this, You *Jefuits* muft be my
Locufts, my *Beuteficaus* to go into the Courts
of all thefe Kingdomes, and fet them all on
a light Fire (in Warring one againft another)
that my Religion (which hath grown very
cold ever fince Unhappy *Luther* call'd the
Pope, Antichrift) may be warmed again
with thofe very *Flames* that I (by you my
Engines) have kindled. You know, *Chrift*
hath made me a *Fifher of Men*, as before,
and I find it beft Fifhing in *Troubled Waters*.
Nay, I am the true *Salamander*, that can beft
                                                    live

live in the Flames, of Foreign and Secular Princes Contentions, *&c.*

The *Third Proposal* was, to *Depose those Kings that will not Truckle*, and to *Expose* their Kingdomes, *primo occupaturo*, the first that can win it, let them wear it, I will warrant the Assault of the Aggressor, *&c.*

The Fourth nimble Trick he Proposed was, saying, Though I have a Thausand more Reaching and Effectual Knacks to offer, yet seeing you know them all so well, 'tis superfluous to mention more, save onely this, which is; *Instar Omnium.* You must in Reducing all others, Begin with that *Stubborn Kingdome of England,* which hath been more fatal to my Tripple Crown than all other Kingdomes, and when you have made a *Breakfast* of that, then make your *Dinner* of this, *&c.* and your *Supper* of that, *&c.* and so *go on* and my *Blessing go with you.*

Thus ended the *Seraphical* or rather *Diabolical* Oration of this *Innocent* Grave old Gentleman that never did, nor ever will do Harm to any.

This done, the Damnable Popish Plot was in all its Parts and Paragraphs contrived,&c. The Romish Fry of *Priests and Jesuits,* (who were soon Hatch'd and grew Fledge under his Holiness's Wing) came Flying over in

great

great Wild-goose Flocks· into *England;* we may suppose they came fully furnished with their *Pick-lccks* of *Pardons,* with their *Pad-lccks* of *Auricular· Confession,* and all other useful Engines to. promote their· Hellish *Project,* the Sum whereof in the general was, to Subvert the Established Government: and Religion of this Kingdom, and to Reduce the same to the *Foppery* of *Popery,* yea, and 'twas concluded at the Consult *(which theſe· Romish, Emiſſaries came to. Accomplish)* that no manner of Tolleration should be granted to any fort of Proteftants; but all ſuch should be Extirpated *Root & Branch,* and if all other means failed, it should be effected by *Fire and Sword.*

The cheif Confpirators, who defigned, and were engaged to carry on this Bloudy project, muft be thus Ranked in a lafting Record.

☞ *Firſt,* The Fountain of thefe Bitter Waters, and Original of all, was this *Prefent Pope Innocent* the 11th, who in the Congregation [*de propaganda. Fide*] confifting of about 350 Perfons, (all fit Tools for the Devils Work) and held about *December 1677.* as foon as he was well warm in *Peter's* Chair, He Plots (even in that cold Seafon) work Hot enough for poor *England:* Then was it He belchd out that *nocent* rather than *Inno-*

cent Oration aforementioned, Declaring further, that this Kingdome was a part of
St. *Peters Patrimony,* and was forfeited to the
Holy See, by the Herefy both of *Prince* and
People, and fo muft be difpofed of as he
thought meet : though this *Pope* was the
primus motor, the *primum mobile,* or great
Wheel that moved all the lower Orbs, and
fet all the lefler Wheels on Work, yet let
us take a fhort view of his Under-Engines,
before we more fully give him his due Character, upon this *laft* (which at the *laft day*
will be a great) *Account* alfo, to wit, his
Plots, as before, his *Cheats,* in the one a
crafty *Fox,* in the other a *cruel Tyger,* and
furely whoever were the Inftruments, the
Members, the Hands and the Feet for Acting
this Bloudy Plot, to Reduce *England* to the
Roman Rotten Religion, we fhall find *Him*
the Head and Principal Agent.   My Defign
is here to fet the Saddle upon the Right
Horfe: 'Tis a Thoufand pitties, that the
petty larceners fhould *be Hang'd* and *Beheaded,*
(though that be no more than what both
Diftributive and *Commutative Juftice* moft
Juftly Required) and the grand Thief (that
fet them all on work) efcape Scot-free. How
many did pity thofe poor mercenary
Rogues that were Executed, for that Inhu-
mane and Cowardly Murther of that Eminent

nent Patriot *Efquire Thinn*, when they faw
Count Connifmark, the great Rogue, (that
fet his filly Vaffals on Work) to be acquitted . but there is a [δι ιη'] a *Vengeance*;
(even in the Judgment of no better than
Barbarians, Act. 28. 4.) *which will not fuffer*
either the *one* or the *other long to live*; becaufe the *God of Juftice* hath peremptorily
faid, that the *Bloudy* and *Deceitful Men fhall
not live out half their days*, Pfal. 55. 23.

Take here a Diftinct Lift and Catalogue
of the *chief* Plotters in this Late and Damnable Plot, and View them from Head to
Foot, from *Top to Toe*, as they ftand Ranked
in our Englifh Records, and Orderly Regiftred for everlafting Remembrance..

First, This *Prefent Pope Innocent the Eleventh* , the *Mafter of all the Mifrule* and
Matchlefs Mifchief : as the Philofopher faith
of *Finis*, 'tis *primus Intentione*, but *ultimus
Executione* ; So muft 1 fay of this *Fino Filth*,
He is the *firft in Intention*, (his Curfed Character being the principal end propofed in
this prefent Difcourfe) yet muft He come
laft in Execution, not onely in the *Method* of
this *Platform*, but alfo (for ought I yet fee)
in the *Meafures* of Gods *Providence* : For
the *Law of Juftice* (compared to the
Cobweb that catches the leffer Flyes, but
cannot keep the great ones, *&c.*) is too

Low and Short Handed (as to Man) to
Reach so High and so Far as the *Great Goff*
of *Rome*, Yet surely *in due Season His Sin*
shall find him out by the great God, *Numb.*
32. 23. unto whom we must leave Him,
for He is the *God of Vengeance, Justice is His,*
and *He will Repay,* Deut. 32. 35. 43.
Rom. 12. 19.

Secondly, *Cardinal H ward,* by Birth both
an *English Man,* and *Brother* to the Great
Duke of Norfolk; So one of the Popes first
and fittest Engines to Betray *England* into
His *Holinesses* Hands, that thereby this *Car-*
dinal might the more Merit Saint *Peters*
Chair upon this Popes Departure from it,
and then this Sweet Bit (our Land) would
prove a Sowceing Augmentation to *Peters*
Patrimony: Therefore, as the Pope was *Lord*
High Admiral in the whole *See* of *Rome;*
So, it was concluded by the *Cabal* in the
Colledg *de propaganda fide,* that this same
English Cardinal, should be his *Vice Admiral,*
and hereupon He was dispatch'd away
from *Rome* to be the *Popes Legatus a Latere,*
or a *None Such Nuncio* into *England,* upon
such an unparalleld Errand, as never any
Embassadour durst undertake, which was to
take possession of *it* in this Popes Name, as
if it had been claps'd into his Hands for
want of either Heir or Possessour, though
Blessed

Bleſſed be God it hath both, and needs none of the *Popes falſe Claims,* or *foul uſurpations;* and to make this Cardinal more brisk in his exploit, the Pope Creates Him *Arch-Biſhop of Canterbury* (as if *there* had been a Vacancy too) and, that *Sees Vaſt· Revenue* being look'd upon as too little a Bribe for ſo Heroick an undertaker, the *Pope* ordains Him Forty Thouſand Crowns *per Annum* out of His own Coffers (where there is *Gold and Silver enough,* &c. Rev. 18. 12, 13.) as a neceſſary ſupplement to that pittiful Arch-Biſhoprick (the Beſt and Richeſt in *England*) that He might be had in more Veneration ; and the better Support His Authoritative Grandieur : And as if this alone were below this *Innocent Harmleſs Pope* (like another *proud Haman*) to lay His Violent Hands onely upon our *Mordecai* (the *Biſhop of Canterbury,* as well as *King Charles the Second*) to Diſpoſſeſs them both of their *Crown* and *Miter,* but He daringly Diſpoſſeſſeth (ſo far as the good will of the evil Beaſt would ſtretch) moſt of our other *Biſhops,* promoting His own Popelings as ſo many *Interlopers* in their places, as Father *Perrot* to *York, Corker* to *London, Whitebread* to *Wincheſter, Strange* to *Durham: Godder* to *Salisbury, Napper* to *Norwich,* &c. I appeal to all thoſe Biſhops (whom this Pope would

would have *turned out* to Grazing, unleſs
they could have *turned in* to Him) whether
His *Name* and His *Nature* do correſpond
well herein, and whether they would not
have had hereupon far greater Reaſon to
brand Him (as in Scripture, *this is*
King Ahaz) ſaying likewiſe, this is *Pope*
Nocent, rather than *Pope Innocent* the *Eleventh*:
All muſt Truckle to *Cardinal Howard* His
Nuncio.

Thirdly, *Johannes Paulus de Oliva*, comes
in next to play his pranks, and as He had
been the Father *General of the Jeſuits* in all
Lands, ſo this *Pope* Conſtitutes *Him* his *Rere-*
Admiral, to *Mann* and to Mannage a right
Romes Great *Man of War*, the *Provincial* of
the *Jeſuits* in *London*, in ſo noble an Attack:
but is Attacking in a Military manner,
proper Work for an *Olivas*, whoſe Name
carries an *Olive Leaf* (that Badg of Peace)
in its Mouth, but it ſeems, He will be like
his Great Maſter, *Pope Nocent Innocent*, there
is *War in his Heart*. Which minds me of a
Story concerning the foregoing *Pope Inno-*
cent the Tenth, who bare for part of his
Arms [*a Dove with an Olive Branch in her*
Mouth] Whereupon our Turn Coat and
Runagate *Doctor Baily* wittily Quibbles upon *Oliva vera*, profoundly perverting it to
Oliverus, and highly Courted that Protector
with

with his *Seraphick* Comparifon of the *Olive*
and *Oliver*. See his Life of *Fisher*, p. 260, 261.
'Tis the genuine Character of a *Jesuit* to
have *Honey* (or the *Olive of Peace*) in *his
Mouth*, and to have defigned (yea Confecrated) Swords and Daggers in his Heart.
Oh *brave Olive*, Oh *brave Oliver*, the han-
dle of the Sword that fhould have been
Sheath'd in our Bowels, Reached to *Rome*,
and was held in this Brave *Olivas* Hand.

Fourthly, *Pedro Jeronimo de Corduba*, Provincial of the Jefuits in *New-Caftle* in *Spain*,
the Pope mufr have here a *Paul* (as His
Third Engine) and a *Peter* (as this Fourth)
engaged with Himfelf herein, though both
Jefuits (without whom no Mifchief in all
Europe can be managed, the *Hand of Joab*
or *Jefuite* is in all) to make this *Damnable*
and *Diabolical Plot* more like *Apoftolical*:
That Work which this Pope cut out for him,
was to be a *Grand Pilot* in his Countrey, and
to give the Plot a lift endways, both with
Money and *Men*, under the notion of Pil-
grims: and where *this* Popifh *Pedro* or *Peter* plaid his pranks like a right Beautifeu to
Sow his Seed of Contention betwixt that
Crown and this, thereby the more to facili-
tate the further Progrefs of the Plot.

Fifthly, *La Chefe* a *Jefuit* too, and Con-
feffor to the *French King* (and fo mufr be
Privy

Privy to all his Royal Designs) *He* was also a *Grand Pilot* in that Countrey, whose hands were directed to Steer a right Course here-in by that conceited Coxcomb, our *Cole-man*, who was hang'd for his pains in Be-traying his own Native Countrey.

Sixthly, Another Jesuite (I have not his Name, and indeed 'tis not worth enquiry) who is Confessour to the *Empercur* of *Ger-many*, must Create Fends betwixt *Him* and our King: That, with all these pretty Di-versions, we might be wheadled into a Ga-zing abroad, while they by their *English Jesuits*, &c. could cut our Throats at Home: Mark here, what a Sacred Num-ber is Six, with them there must be Six of Forreign Affistants (the Number of the Beast is Three Sixes as before) and still *Jesuits* every where must be the *Inftru-ments* of Cruelty, though the Pope be the hand to Improve them : I the less wonder at this, since I Read that pallage in the Jesuit *Muffeius*, writing the Life of *Igna-tius Loyala* their Founder, He there Inge-riously confelleth, that their *Father Imitated the Devil in ufing Tricks to Convert* (or rather *Pervert*) *Disciples*, &c. You may Swear, that all the *Jesuits* do *Patrizars* and will *Try* the *Devils Tricks* with the best of *Juglers*, &c.

But

But are our Jefuits in *England* afleep all this while? No, the Pope hath *Domeſtick* Tools as well as *Forreign*.

This Popes Domeſtick Engines employed here, were Thefe

Firſt, The *Provincial of the Jefuits* , for the Time being in *England*, who was *White-Bread*, who would have made Brownbread and Brann of us , but he *fell into his own Pit*, &c.

Secondly, The *Benedictine Monks* at the *Savoy*. The Duke of *Savoys* Country was call'd *Malvoy*, becaufe it was- pefterd fo notorioufly with Theeves as made it *Mala-Via* or *Malvoy*, that is, a *Dangerous Paſſage*, but when the Thieves were Rooted out, its Name was changed into *Salvoy* or *Savoy* , the way *thence* to *Somerfet-houfe*, makes the Application more eafie.

Thirdly, The *Jefuits* and *Seminary Prieſts*, who were *Sowing* their *Tares among* the Wheat (like the *Envious one* their Father*) all over the Land, they being about the Number of *Eighteen Hundred*, a large black Regiment under Roman Colours.

Fourthly, Many *Lay-Papiſts both of the Nobility* and *Gentry* (too well known to need naming) who had all Commiſſions Sealed by Brave *Oliva* aforementioned, both for Civil and Military Employ, and fent them by by *this Pope*; as the Higheſt Marks of his Favour.

Fifthly , *Multitudes* , *Multitudes of the Lay-Papiſts* among the *Commonalty.* Even all the Papiſts in *England* could not chuſe. but be Engaged in ſo Glorious and Merito-rious a Matter ; and this is the more pro-bable, If not only their General Principles, Imbibed with their Religion, but alſo the Popes particular Teſt (for Anathematizing us Hereticks) Impoſed Univerſally on them, be but well conſidered.

Sixthly, For ſtill we muſt have the Six in Adoration of Six Hundred Sixty Six, *&c. All the Engliſh Covents beyond Sea,* (as St. *Omors*, &c.) muſt be almoſt drain'd Dry, and Tranſported *Incognito's* hither, to Cor-roberate the better carrying on of the Ca-tholick Cauſe, which was now become as Catholick as their *Religion,* having likewiſe all the moſt Eminent of the Popiſh Clergy in *Europe* Engaged to help at a Dead Lift, and to Lift *England* to *Rome.* Hereby this Plot became the Unanimous Act of the whole *Romiſh* Church, whoſe *Infallible* and *Innocent* Head (this Pope) Adjur'd them to it, upon the forfeiture of their Fathers Bleſſing. Though we may not Imagine every Individual Popeling could know the whole Intrigue (for there might be a

K   Wheel

Wheel within a Wheel). yet in the Lump
they pay to this Pope their *Blind Obedience*,
however the Guilt both of the parts, and
of the whole, falls upon the *Innocent* Con-
ſcience of this Pope, which all his *Holy Water* cannot waſh off, and make him as *Innocent* as his Name, ſhould he Conjure *Tibur*
it ſelf.

Now when His Holineſs had thus well
furniſhed his Holy Cauſe with *Men* (a double Set of Sixes, a *Jury* of Twelve, I cannot ſay, *All Good Men and True*, No, not
ſo much as the *Foreman himſelf*) His next
Care is to be ſupply'd with *Money*, the *Sinews* of His *Holy War*, and though his own
private Exchequer be *Puteus In exhauſtus* (as
he once ſaid of *England*, when it was his
Aſs to Ride on; and therefore would fain
beſtride her ſoft Back again,) an *Inexhau-
ſtible Fountain*, yet the Old Crafty Fox liked
better to get ſome Bearers, well knowing
that many Hands make lighter Work. Hereupon by his *Apoſtolical Command*, as well
as *Example*. A Vaſt and Prodigious *Fund*
was quickly Erected for ſo Great and Pious
a Work.

Firſt, The *Pope himſelf*, to be a good Pattern to others, conveys into his Sacred Trea-
ſury by *Paulus de Oliva*, or *Paul Olive*, *Ele-
ven Thouſand Crowns*, I wonder He made it

not

not even *Twelve*,   and the *Crown's, Pounds* ;
His own full Coffers *Revel.* 18. 12. might
well enough have born it besides ;   the Re-
gaining of *England* to His Revenue would
well   enough   have   Countervail'd   that
Cost.

Secondly, The *Catholick King* (His Eldest
Son) of *Spain* shames his *Holy Father*, in
Advancing Ten Thousand Pounds by *Peter*
Jeronimus ; thus his *Indian* Gold was Expend-
ed.

Thirdly, His *Most Christian Son of France*
(to shew himself the better *Christian*,   or
rather *Antichristian*,) Advanceth Ten Thousand Pound more by Father *Le Cheese*, what
a shame it is,   that His Holiness should be
out done by both his Sons, when it was pe-
culiarly His Cause, and He would have Run
away with the Profit.

Fourthly, I wonder we hear nothing of
the *Emperors Charity*, was it because he was
too *Nigardly*,   or because the *Male-Contents*
of *Hungary* kept his Coffers Empty ;   however,   divers considerable Sums were trans-
mitted to *Coleman* by Foreign Ministers,
among whom, *He* from *Germany* might be
one.

Fifthly, But the *English Jesuits* (suppo-
sing the *Emperor* to be too *Narrow Soul'd*,)
Ex Abundanti, supply'd all Defects, they
                      K 2   having

· having Threescore Thousand Pound *per An-*
num, Estate in Land here, and an Hundred
Thousand Pound Ready Cash, a constant
Running Stock in the way of their *Trade*
which (you know) is the *Mystery of Ini-*
quity.

. *Sixthly,* The *Benedictine Monks* (not to
be thrust out as Rotten) contribute out of
their Blessed Treasure, Six Thousand Pound
to purchase the Popes *Benediction,* whom
they also exceeded in their Benevolence, *&c.*

· *Seventhly,* God Bless us, here's the Third
Six again, and so we have got the *exact*
Number of the Beast, Six, and Six, and Six,
or Six Hundred Sixty Six, and to make up
this Number compleat, the *English Catholick*
(as well as *Roman*) *Grandees* were free
Contributors of most *Ample Benevolencies* to
this so Great and so Glorious a Work.

No sooner had this *Innocent* Pope thus
provided Himself (though He as to his part,
comes off but *Stingily*) with *quantum suf-*
ficit (or rather *suffocat,* as to Justice *God-*
frey) both of *Men* and *Money:* He then
sends forth His hungry *Beagles* to Hunt the
harmless Hare, that never gave them the
least provocation : but He *must* do it, 'tis
.the *nature* of the *Beast* to worry the Harmless, and 'tis the *custome* (which is a second
rature) of this *Innocent* Pope to be notoriously *Nocent* to the *Innocent.*   The

.; The *Firft Innocent*, He Aſſaults with his greedy Hounds, is no leſs than *our King* (God Bleſs Him) *Grove* and *Pickering* are hired to ſhoot Him, *Conyers* and *Anderton* to ſtab Him, *four Iriſh Ruffians* to *Godfrey* Him, *Sir George Wakeman* to poyſon Him : *Out of the way with Him, any way* (they cry) ſince He will not *comply with our Plot.*

. *Secondly*, The *Duke of York* ſhall fare no better, unleſs He will turn Tenant to this *Innocent* Pope for his *Kingdom*, as well as for his *Religion*, and pardon the Murtherers of his Brother, the Burners of the City, *&c.* and the Maſſacrers of the People, *&c.*

Thirdly, Becauſe their Horrid and Helliſh Plot had taken *Wind* by *Doctor Oats*'s Depoſitions given in to *Juſtice Godfrey* (whereby their Bloudy Deſigns, both of Murdering the *King* and the *Duke of York* too, If he would not comply, and upon His *Majeſties Murther*, of Firing *Weſtminſter*, *Wapping*, *Rotherith* and *Southwark*, as they had done *London*, and to lay all upon the *Presbyterians*, &c. as likewiſe of making a *General Maſſacre* at the ſame time by a ſecret liſted Army of Five Hundred Thouſand Cut-Throats, whereof the Lord *Bellaſis* was to be General, *&c.* were all Diſcovered) this *good Magiſtrate* muſt have his Mouth ſtoped from telling Tales, *&c.* wherein the Pope

ſuccee-

ſucceeded ſo far as to make this Man the *Firſt Martyr of our Religion, and a fair Ranſom of our Realm.*

The like was Attempted upon *Juſtice Arnold,* though no other Crime was found in either, ſave a faithful Diſcharge of their Oath and Duty. Nor againſt *Juſtice Pye* neither, yet *Bodnam* the Papiſt prevail'd to knock down his *Clay-Cruſt* with his Bill, whereby this *good Pye* (a ſerviceable Diſh in *Hereford-ſhire*) was Deſtroyed.

Fourthly, The *Popes Agents* (being now Fleſh'd in Proteſtants Bloud, yet unable to *ſtiſle the Plot,* when it once was Declared by both Houſes of Parliament that there was a Traiterous Deſign of the Pope to Subject this Kingdom to his Tyrannical Government, by theſe Five pernicious Lords in the *Tower,* whereof *Stafford* lately Executed was, &c.) do then club their Wits, not onely with this *Pope* (the Devils Eldeſt Son) but even with the *Devil* himſelf, how they might handſomly *Sham* it, and this they labour in the very Fire to Accompliſh.

Fifthly, Then began they to play their Popiſh pranks in *Blaſting* the *Kings Evidence,* Sir *Dennis Aſhburnham,* the Saint *Omers Boys,* are brought in to Accuſe *Doctor Oats* of *Perjury,* as *Lane* and *Osborn* did of *Sodomy,* the like *pranks againſt Prance, Bedloe, Dugdale,*

dale, &c. but their Bowl Runs not here
without a Rub for their Deſign of Subborn-
ing *Alderman Brook* and Captain *Bury,* being Diſcovered, this Diſcover'd alſo that all
the aforeſaid Tools were but the *Popes* or the
Devils Trunks through which he ſpake, as
he uſed to do in his *Dumb Images,* which
the Father of Lyes taught to ſay what he
liſted, yet muſt be his *Oracles.*

Sixthly, They, being Non-plus'd herein
alſo by the Over-ruling Hand of God, begin new Methods by the Popes Advice
(and indeed, what ſhould direct Hands and
Feet but the Head) then thought of ſhift-
ing the Plot from their own ſhoulders by
Forging ſeveral *Sham-Plots,* all to be Fa-
thered upon the Proteſtants : thus at a
pinch they are *Ingenioſe nequam* , wickedly
witty.

Heu quantum ſubitis caſibus Ingenium.

Yet this was but to new Vamp a pair of
their old Boots, for that Impious Pope *Pius*
the Fifth, taught his Popiſh Prieſts, that
when they had by the Powder Plot blown
up the King (*James*) Lords and Com-
mons, to Father that filthy Fact upon the
Puritans : the Father of Lyes is put hard
to his Trumps , when he is ſo low Run,
that

that he hath no new Tricks in his Tinkers
Budget to ſtop holes with , but is forced to
bring forth his old Baſſoold Stratagems.
However He is Reſolved to drive this Tinkers nail (new pointed) ſo far as it would
go with his Hammer.

In *Order* to this, They ſtart many *Sham-*
plots, wherewith they indeed began betimes,
even in 1661 (as Captain *Yarranton* Demon-
ſtrates, when the Crown was ſcarce warm
upon our *King Charles* his Head : but that
and all other Succeſſively, were but low
Games compared to this, for then they had
not ſuch a Damnable Plot Diſcovered to
Palliate as now, even this Plot of Plots that
was Hatched at *Rome* as ſoon as this *Innocent*
Pope ſtorm'd *Peter's* Chair, his *Miter* was
ſcarce warm upon his Head (put upon him
in the Year 1676.) but preſently the Devil
enters into him (as if he had taken *Judas's*
Sop) and ſets both his *Head* and his *Heart*
to contrive this Bloudy Deſign, which for
two full Years (like that *ſtrange River* Related in Hiſtory) Ran underground, before
it brake forth and was Diſcovered in the
Year 1678. Now when that Devil and his
Deeds of Darkneſs was brought to Light
(though long wrap'd up in *Samuels* Mantle)
by the Father of Lights, who always over-
ſhoots Satan in in his own Bow, theſe white
Witches

Witches would fain Conjure him down with multiplyd Sham-plots : Indeed,one begetting another *Corruptio Unius* was *Generatio Alterius.*

The *First* was, The *Clapping up of Mr.* Clapool *into the Tower,* before their plot was Difcovered, that they might have him at Hand to Father the Kings Murder upon; fo foon as he fhould fall by their Hands, whereas all the Treafon that can be charg'd upon this modeft Gentleman, is, that he hath led a Retired Life for many Years, and onely feekt to betray the Secrets of Nature by hard Study, as alfo that he Marryed *Olivers Jewel,* which render'd him more fit to Faften their Defigns upon.

The *Second* was, A Raifing of the Report, that *Juftice Godfrey* was a Papift (one of their Creatures faid fo much to my felf) and that he was Murdered by the Proteftants, *&c.* This, by *Nevils* means, was made the common Difcourfe in every Coffehoufe, to amufe the Nation, and to give them a Diverfion from the Papifts. The now Ho-neft Mr. *Dangerfield* knows it to be true.

Of the fame Bran was a later Report that Juftice *Godfrey* Hangd himfelf, for which *N. T.* was Pillory'd, both could not be true, if the one, then not the other, whereas nei-ther is true, for he neither Hangd himfelf, nor dyed he by Proteftants but by Papifts Hands :

Hands: ſtill the Death of one Sham-plot gave Life to another, and one Bafled begat another to the end of the Chapter.

The time would fail (as Room I am ſure doth) to Reckon all *Romes Plots.*

· The *Third* was (to omit *Netervils* endeavouring to Suborn Captain *Bury* and Alderman *Brooks,* &c.) The Duke of *Buck.* was an Eye-fore for ſaying (I ſuppoſe) he would never turn Papiſt, *till they* can eat up the Devil, as, they ſay, they do God in their Hoſt.

For this they firſt Accuſe him of *Treaſon,* and this failing, of *Sodomy.*

The *Fourth* was, The Earl of *Shaftsbury* was their greateſt ſtumbling Block, becauſe His Sagacity had ſo oft Countermined their Deviliſh Deſigns, Hereupon, Plots upon Plots were laid againſt his Life: both by Men and Women, in City and Country.

· The *Fifth* was, Sir *William Waller* had (while in Commiſſion) been a Thorn in their Sides, for daily Ferreting the Foxes out of their Holes, where they had Earth'd themſelves, and openly Condemning their Trumperies to the Flames of a *Purgatory*-fire above ground : no wonder then, if they at that time ſought to blaſt his Reputation, as they (to wit, *Monſon,* whom he had committed to *Newgate*) and *Nevil*, aforementioned,

(alias

(*alias Paine*) do now feek to Deftroy his Life, the Prefervation whereof the *whole Nation,* yea, the whole *Proteftant* Intereft are obliged to Pray for, He being an Active Inftrument in Gods Hand for the Preferva-tion of both.

But the *Sixth* (and ftill this *Miftery of Iniquity* Runs all in *Sixes* both in the *Real* and in the *Sham-plots,* in the *former* and in the *latter* Diftribution.) was a *Plot of Plots,* a Wickednefs with a Witnefs indeed : which (in fome fenfe) was worfe than either the *Irifh* or *Parifian Maffacre,* wherein good Men onely loft their lives, but herein they muft lofe their *Reputations* too, as Branded with Rebellion to Pofterity . 'Twas worfe than the Cruelty of *Nero,* who only wifh'd all the People had but one Neck , that *He* might cut them all off at one Blow : but here was more than a bare *wifh,* a *crafty endeavour* to blow up all the Proteftant Lords (the Duke of *Monmouth,* &c.) All the Proteftant *Gentry* and *Yeamonry* in *City* and *Country* at one Blaft, by fixing High Treafon upon them all Univerfally : and when the Knife was at our Throats, God fent Sir *William Waller* to turn up the bottou of *Mad-dame Celliers Meal-Tub,* where all the Bran of this Brutifh Intreague was Difcovered, *Cum multis aliis quæ nunc perfcribere longum eft.* Thefe

⁚ Thefe and a Thoufand more pretty *Inno-cent* Pranks hath this Pope *Innocent* the *Eleventh* plaid in poor *England,* though not in his *Perfon,* yet by his *Proxy,* whatever His Slaves and Vaffals have Acted here, even *Matchlefs Villanies,* All have been by an *Implicit Faith,* and by a *Blind Obedience* to his *Apoftolical (* or rather *Apoftatical)* Commands ; but furely that Servant who will be Hang'd for his Mafter, or for his Mafters Fault more than his own, muft needs have more of *Blind Charity,* than of a *Solid Judgment.*

⁚ 𝕂☞ One would Admire, that any Humane Breaft could be fo Capacious as to contain in it fo much *Villanous Venom* as this *Innocent Pope* hath poured out upon *England* ; but is here all ? No, *Scotland, France, Ireland* and *Holland,* yea, and all other Proteftant Countries, muft likewife be Wounded with the Poifonful Sting of this *Fiery Flying Serpent,* this *Great Red Dragon,* Mounted aloft upon the Higheft Theatre in the Chriftian World, hath his profpect into all thefe places, and, as if He *True Bafilisk,* Kills down-right with his very *Looks,* His *Looks* are Top-full of Fafcination. To tell diftinctly how he hath Bewitched with his bare *Looks* all thofe Lands aforenamed, would Require another Volum. Take here only

only a very Brief Landskip hereof, which yet may serve to satisfie, that this pretended Head is Top-full of Poison, and this Catholick Head of the Church Transfuseth a Fatal Poison into all the parts of the Body; his *Venom* is as *Universal* as his *Headship*.

As *First*, For *Scotland*, He sent several Jesuits to Preach there under the Notion of Presbyterians, who Induftrioufly Blew up the Coals of Difcontent among that People, knowing that *Oppreffion maketh Wife Men Mad*, Aggravating to them their Unbearable Burdens under Epifcopal Tyranny, exciteing them to Vindicate their Religion and Liberty with the Sword, and promifing them in the *Popes* Name, That they fhould be Affifted with Eight Thoufand Catholicks to overturn the Government.

Oh how did this Pope Laugh in his Lawn Sleeves, to fee himfelf fo *Succefsful*. See Dr. *Oats Narrative, Art.* 1, 74, 11.

Secondly, As to *France*, How far this *Innocent* Pope hath been *Nocent there*, How far his *Tincture* of *Lucifer* hath turn'd his *Chriftian* Son into *Antichriftian*, may be Legibly Read, even in Capital Letters, in the *Bloody Whales* upon the Backs of the *Hugonots*, but moft of all in that *Deteftable Teft*, which wounds not their *Bodies* only, but their *Souls* alfo; unlefs they will *Abjure* the Prote

stant

ftant Religion, *Anathematize* all Proteftants, this·hath Turn'd out of *France* many Thoufands of the Tendereft part of that People into Foreign Countries,·though *it* be fo Diametrically   contrary   to   the·Sacred *Edicts of* N*ants,* fo folemnly Sworn to by the *French King.* Yet this Pope,·by·his Omnipotency, dare Abfolve him from this Oath, and Undertakes to make Sin a Duty. See Sir *William Waller's Account of the prefent State of the Proteftants there.* ·And fee·alfo, *The Politicks of France.* And whether all this Conteft betwixt the *Father* and the *Son,* about the *Regalia's,* be not all a Juggle, (feeing the poor·Proteftants are among Hands fo fevearly Perfecuted,·and peftilent Jefuits fo Cordially Embraced,) Time.will Declare.

·*Thirdly,* As to *Ireland ,* Dr. *Oats* Depofeth, *Narrat.* pag.65,66.That this·*Innocent Pope* fent his *Bloudy Irifh Hounds, Commiffion's, Arms,* and *Eight Hundred Thoufand Crowns,* that. they might cut the Throats of the Proteftants again, as they had done by another *Innocent* Popes Order in One Thoufand Six Hundred Forty One. The Death of the Duke of *Ormond* fhould lead this Popifh Dance, the Pope loofes of his Bloud-Hounds (Four Jefuits) who Undertook to Difpatch the Duke, Twenty Five Thoufand

sand *Irish* were to Rise, and play their Old
Bloudy Game, wherein they were Experi-
enced, and Artificial Gamesters. These
were to Join with a *French Army* to be
Landed there, and as good Gamesters of
that Kind as they, so fall on to their Old
Trade of Massacring, &c. Yea, some of
those *Irish Cattel* had a Dispensation from
this Pope to take the *Oaths* of *Allegiance*
and *Supremacy*, provided they promise to
Betray their Garrisons, and other Trusts:
So that when you see a Papist swallow those
Oaths, you may Swear 'tis with such a
proviso, He hath some Trust or other to Betray.

Fourthly, Holland, There this *Innocent*
Pope hath set his Foul Foot (of the *Beast*:)
to purpose, in sending his *Most Christian Son*,
most Unchristianly to Scourge them for
their Heresie, and to over-run their Countrey with his Rapacious Army ; and had
not God Almighty put an Hook into the
Jaw of that Proud *Leviathan* at *Utrecht*,
He had laid their Land under an Absolute
Desolation. To say nothing of *His* Intrigue-
ing Influences to plunge *them* and *us*
into a War to Wast and Weaken each other,
that He might the easier worry *us* both :
To say nothing of *Hungary* and other parts
of *Germany*, nor of the Three *Northern*

Crowns ;

Crowns ; in all which he hath throughly tryed the fame Trufty Tricks of *Divide, and Command,* &c.

Yet while this Pope is thus *Malevolent* and *Mifchievous* abroad (embroiling all Countries with his Contagious Evomitions) He is all this while Mighty Magnificent and Magifterial at Home., ftrutting about in that *Splendour and Grandeur,* as if He were more than a *Mortal Man* on *Earth,* one of the *Immortal Angels* of *Heaven,* Refembling the *Angelical Nature,* not onely in *Innocency* in his Name *Innocent,* but alfo in *Luftre and Glory* , as to his Garb and Deportment: Grant Him to be one of the Angels Order, yet undervalue him not, by reckoning him among the Inferior Rank. No, let him be Reputed no lefs than *proud Lucifer,* a Prince or Principality among them, &c. *Ifa.* 14.14. As to his *Innocency* ; Angel like, I can fay little of it, and fure I am nor no body elfe. (unlefs fome of his Sycophants who can be content to lick up his *Slaver,* as once one *Parafite* did a Tyrants) no further than his Name [*Innocent*] will be the Guarranty: To be *Nocent* in *Nature* (as the premiffes have proved him) and to be *Innocent* in Name, is to make himfelf a compleat lump of Contradiction: However this *Whore of Babylon* can exactly Imitate *Solomons Whore*

in

in *wiping her Mouth*, and saying I have not
done thofe mifchiefs in all thofe Lands aforementioned : But as to this Splendour and
Glory, Angel-like, I have more to fay than
I have room for, as to his *Roman Grandeur*,
never was *Jaddus* (the *High Prieft* of the
Jews) fo Richly Array'd for *Glory and
Beauty*, when *Great Alexander* met him and
fell down to Worfhip him for a god, as this
Roman Pontifex in all his pompious pontificalibus is, either fitting in his Chair of State,
or ftanding upright, or ftrutting about. The
Prophet *Ezekiel* moft graphically Defcribes
*this Anointed Cherub, that Seats himfelf in the
Holy Mountain of God,&fits as God*(that is a de-
greeabove an *Angel*)*covering himfelf with every
pretious Stone,* the *Rubys,* the *Diamonds,* the
Jafper, the *Saphire* and *Emerauld,* &c. *Ezek.*
28. 2. 13, 14, 15, to 20. Oh what a glittering and glorious Scarlet coloured Beaft
is this, thus bedeckt with Radiant Jewels.
No wonder if they give him this Canting
Courtfhip [*Thou art the prime of all Bifhops,
the Heir of the Apoftles, an Abel for primacy*
(fure I am, not for Religion) *a Noah for
Government* (not for Righteoufnefs) *an A-
braham for Patriarkfhip* (not for Piety) *a
Melchifedeck for Order, an Aaron for Dignity,
a Mofes for Authority, a Samuel for Judica-
ture, a Peter for Power,* yea, *a Chrift for*
    L   *Unction,*

Unction, but none of them for *Holiness*,
though that be his Title : No wonder if
his pickthanks go yet higher, in calling
him [*their Lord God, their Creator in whom
they muſt Believe, and whom they muſt Obey
upon pain of Damnation*] no wonder if
they ſay to this their God three times [*Oh
Thou that takeſt away the Sins of the World,
have Mercy on us. Thou canſt make a Sin to
be no Sin, & contrà*] No wonder if Popelings *Kiſs the great Toe* of their *Great God*,
in a Country where God hath Toes, which
Moſes (who came neareſt him) could not
Diſcern, and much leſs Kiſs, *Deut.* 4.12;15.
No wonder if Kings and Emperours *hold
the Stirrop*, to this God, when weary with
walking, and would Ride; one Beaſt upon
the back of another, no wonder if *Odeſchalcho* thought his Name too baſe for a *God*, as
Octavian did, when choſen Pope at Eighteen
Years old, caſt off his *Name* becauſe *Heath-
niſh*, and calls himſelf *John* the *Thir-
teenth*, but he proved ſuch *a God* as uſed
to drink Healths to the Devil, and in his
Diceing would Pray, that *Jupiter, Venus*,
and all the Devils would help him.
This was a *Mad Jack* indeed, and as *Bad
a   ſould be All good.

To conclude, come my Country-men, how can you like to Worſhip ſuch a God, (who is rather a *Devil* Incarnate, or the *Devils Patriarch*) can you ſtoop to *kiſs his ſtinking Toe,* can you *hold his Stirrup* (as too many are doing) till he get upon your own Backs and Ride you to the Devil, Grave *Biſhop Uſhar* feard a Maſſacre approaching, and that this very Pope would be the chief Agent in it? Can you Court in a bloudy Villain, who will certainly cut your Throats? Can you like to Trade with ſuch a Cheat (that is as *Crafty* as *Cruel,* having as much of the Fox as of the Lyon) in his *Traſh and Trumpery* afore mentioned? This Pope had great hopes of Reentry into *England* by his hopeful Plot., hereupon *Cottingtons* Bones were brought to be Buried *here,* to take poſſeſſion of it as *Jacob* did in like matner of *Canaan:* Indeed, the *late Comet* frighted him into ſuch a *cold Sweat,* as nothing but a Dutch Stove could bring warmth into him again, and the *Cockatrice* laid by the Prophetick Hen in *Campideglis* Garden ſtun'd him a little; But now he Recovered with *warm Cloaths* and hot Cordials again, yet I hope 'tis but a lightning before his fall: God forbid, that the Imperial Crown of *England* ſhould again Truckle to the Miter

any

and Tripple Crown of this Pope: *Erafmus* Satyrical Drollery prevailed againft the Pope, as well as *Luthers Argumentative Gravity*, I wifh the like Efficacy to this Difcourfe, and let all good People fay, Amen.

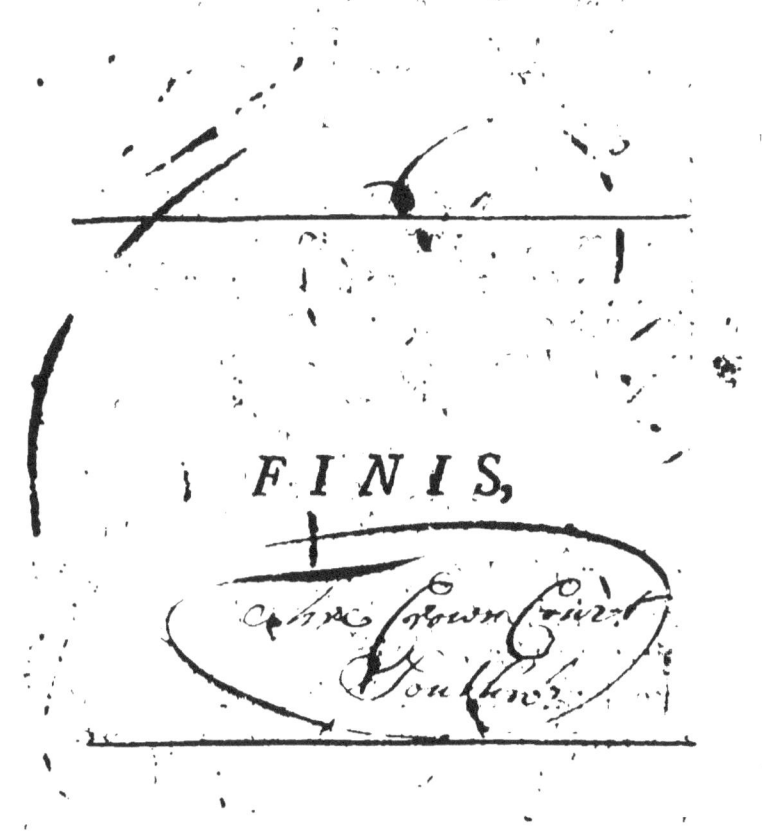

FINIS,